"Betwene Ernest and Game"

American University Studies

Series IV
English Language and Literature
Vol. 110

PETER LANG
New York • Bern • Frankfurt am Main • Paris

Alexandra Hennessey Olsen

"Betwene Ernest and Game"

The Literary Artistry of the *Confessio Amantis*

PETER LANG
New York • Bern • Frankfurt am Main • Paris

Library of Congress Cataloging-in-Publication Data

Olsen, Alexandra Hennessey
  Betwene Ernest and game : the literary artistry of the Confessio amantis / Alexandra Hennessey Olsen.
    p. cm. — (American university studies. Series IV, English language and literature ; vol 110)
  Includes bibliographical references.
  1. Gower, John, 1325?-1408. Confessio amantis. 2. Gower, John, 1325?-1408 – Style. 3. English language – Middle English, 1100-1500 – Style. 4. Love in literature   I. Title. II. Series.
  PR1984.C63047   1990   821'.1 – dc20   89-13292
  ISBN 0-8204-1141-8   CIP
  ISSN 0741-0700

CIP-Titelaufnahme der Deutschen Bibliothek

Olsen, Alexandra Hennessey:
"Betwene ernest and game" : the literary artistry of the Confessio Amantis / Alexandra Hennessey Olsen. – New York ; Bern ; Frankfurt am Main ; Paris: Lang, 1989.
  (American University Studies: Ser. 4, English Language and Literature; Vol. 110)
  ISBN 0-8204-1141-8

NE: American University Studies / 04

© Peter Lang Publishing, Inc., New York 1990

All rights reserved.
Reprint or reproduction, even partially, in all forms such as microfilm, xerography, microfiche, microcard, offset strictly prohibited.

Printed by Weihert-Druck GmbH, Darmstadt, West Germany

To my sisters,
Victoria L. Mason and Veronica L. Hennessey

Acknowledgements

I would like to thank Professors C. David Benson, Michael D. Cherniss, and Raymond P. Tripp, Jr., who read this book in manuscript, made helpful comments on the draft, and recommended it for publication. The errors that remain in it are purely my own.

I should also like to thank the following:

Bouma's Boekhuis N.V. for permission to quote from *Historia Apollonii Regis Tyri*, ed. G. A. A. Kortekaas, Mediaevalia Groningana, vol. 3;

The Council of the Early English Text Society for permission to quote from the works of John Gower edited by G. C. Macaulay;

In Geardagum for permission to reprint "The Literary Impact of the Pun in Middle English Poetry," which appeared in *In Geardagum* 7 (1986): 17-36, and which appears in expanded form as chapter three, "Puns and the Language of Poetry in the *Confessio Amantis*."

Finally, I would like to thank the Research and Creative Work Fund of the University of Denver which made the publication of this book possible, and the following people at the University of Denver:

Carolyn Bolden, Senior Software Specialist, for her help in the conversion of Wordperfect 4.1 to 5.0 and her help in printing the text;

Christine Boni of The College, who, with the permission of Dean Charles Cortese, helped me experiment with the laser printer;

my colleague, Margaret E. Whitt, who helped me with proofreading the manuscript;

and above all, Cynthia Spears, secretary of the Department of English, who taught me to use Wordperfect and helped me overcome the difficulties of using it.

Documentation

I have used the new MLA documentation style in this study, with some small adjustments. Works of poetry are cited by author, page number, and line number, except in the case of poems by Gower. For the *Confessio Amantis* and "To King Henry IV: In Praise of Peace," I have used the EETS edition of *The English Works of John Gower* and have cited the former by book and line number and the latter by line number. In the case of quotations from the Latin marginalia and from the editor's introduction and notes, I have cited the volume and page number. For Gower's other works, I have cited the appropriate work and page number or book and line number to refer to *The Complete Works of John Gower, vol. I: The French Works* and *vol. 4: The Latin Works*. In the list of Works Cited, I have used abbreviations of the titles of common periodicals, following the style of the *MLA Bibliography*.

Table of Contents

Introduction — 1

Chapter One
Reading the *Confessio Amantis*:
The Analogue of Dante's *Vita Nuova* — 5

Chapter Two
The Grammar of the *Confessio Amantis* — 19

Chapter Three
Puns and the Language of Poetry
in the *Confessio Amantis* — 33

Chapter Four
Linguistics and Literary Structure:
Metonymy and the *Confessio Amantis* — 53

Chapter Five
Type-Scenes and the Structure of Narrative:
The Sea Voyages in the Tale of Appolinus — 71

Chapter Six
"Of Storial Thyng":
The Relationship of the Tales
of Gower and Chaucer Reconsidered — 87

Conclusion — 103

Notes — 105

Works Cited — 115

Index — 128

Introduction

The literary works of John Gower have had a long and intriguing critical history. The *Confessio Amantis*, his most acclaimed work, was widely read in the Middle Ages, and around "forty complete manuscripts survive and there are extracts in many others, a number that suggests that it did not fall too far short of the *Canterbury Tales* in popularity and far outstripped Chaucer's other works. It was translated into Spanish, and printed by Caxton in 1483 and by Berthelette in 1532 and 1554" (Cooper, 39; see Manly and Russell on the Portuguese translation of the *Confessio*). Thereafter, the *Confessio* fell into disrepute, and it was not printed in Elizabethan England; during recent centuries, Gower has been disparaged by readers, scholars, and critics who assume that he was a lesser literary artist than Chaucer.[1] Indeed, some scholars simply criticize Gower adversely in order to aggrandize Chaucer's reputation, and many judgments are asserted rather than proved by a close reading of Gower or a careful comparison of Gower and Chaucer. Even a thorough and thoughtful scholar like Donald R. Howard has commented that Gower "wanted to have 'high' seriousness and it ended in drabness. Chaucer found in his ironic style a way to approach seriousness and avoid pretentiousness and solemnity" (51). Close comparison of the works themselves, however, can lead to judgments not necessarily detrimental to Gower. Indeed, Rosemary Woolf points out that "Chaucer's apostrophe to Gower as 'moral' and Coleridge's reference to the 'innate kindliness' of Chaucer's nature have had a distorting effect upon much modern criticism of these two authors" (221). She compares specifics in the works of the two and argues that "it many be more illuminating to reverse the labels and call them kindly Gower and moral Chaucer" (223).

Recent work on the *Confessio* has shown the accuracy of Woolf's judgment about Gower's kindly nature. For example, Linda Barney Burke shows that the *Confessio* has "a tone of mellowness, sensitivity, and compassion for the limitations of human nature" ("Women" 238), and Derek Pearsall notes Gower's humane treatment of women (see "Gower's Narrative Art" 481). As a result, it no longer seems necessary to begin a study of Gower with an apology, as John H. Fisher did as recently as 1964, when he said that "Gower did not have a profound philosophic mind nor was he a great literary artist" (v) but that Gower is nevertheless worth reading. Other critics have re-examined the praise improperly bestowed on Gower by his admirers; John Lawlor, for example, has discussed C. S. Lewis' claim that Gower is basically a romantic poet and has concluded that such a reading exemplifies a critical tendency to "substitute a poem of the reader's own invention for the poem that lies before him" (138).

Readers have come to realize that the critical assertion that Chaucer's poetry is superior to Gower's "is too facile, and their tone betrays an *inability* to respond to and enjoy" [Gower's work] (Farnham, 165) [italics mine]. Some recent critics have discussed Gower and Chaucer together without devaluing Gower, as may be exemplified by Judith Davis Shaw who believes that Gower has a "steady vision" that Chaucer lacks as well as "ironic subtleties" and "soul-searching sobriety" ("*Lust* and *Lore*" 120), and Robert F. Yeager, who discusses Gower's treatment of the Deadly Sin of Gluttony (see "Aspects of Gluttony") to illuminate Chaucer's attitude thereto in the *Canterbury Tales*. Helen Cooper finds much to praise in Gower's work: the fact that Gower found "a balance between frame and stories that can provide coherence without also imposing the monotony of a single theme" (38), the fact that "Gower's regular octosyllabics maintain an unvarying level of poetic competence" (39), and the fact that the *Confessio* "is unquestionably a remarkable achievement" (39), even though the *Canterbury Tales* is a greater one in her eyes.

Piero Boitani calls Gower "one of the greatest intellectuals and artists, as well as one of the chief critical minds, of his time" (*English Medieval Narrative* 117), and his sensitive reading of Gower's works typifies that of recent scholars who have read Gower's entire *oeuvre* rather than merely selections therefrom.[2] Some of the revision of the opinion concerning Gower results from the application of sound critical principles to his work. In the Introduction to a recent volume of essays, Alastair J. Minnis maintains that the authors of the essays in the volume have made "a conscious effort ... to avoid the old ruts" (1) and bring "a special expertise or neglected body of knowledge to bear on the interpretative problems" (1) of the *Confessio*. The essays represent historical scholarship--the effort to understand a writer in terms of his own age[3]--at its most productive: John A. Burrow, for example, uses medieval ideas about the Ages of Man to illuminate the *Confessio* ("Portrayal"), whereas Minnis (see "Moral Gower"), Paul Miller, and Charles Runacres discuss the *Confessio* in terms of "the literary theory and conventions contemporaneous with Gower" (Minnis, "Introduction" 2).

Such historical scholarship demonstrates that Gower's reputation in his own day and through the mid-sixteenth century was well deserved, and it should inspire the unprejudiced to turn to Gower with the attention he merits. Nevertheless, historical scholarship largely addresses itself to those who believe that works of a given period are worth reading rather than to modern readers who argue that particular works are of interest only to historians and antiquarians. There is, therefore, a need to explain why Gower's works deserve a place in the canon of English literature in terms of their value to modern readers *as literature*, to explain the literary artistry thereof without neglecting the tools of historical scholarship.[4] In order to illuminate the artistry of the *Confessio* and demonstrate that the entire poem is of interest in the late twentieth century, one needs to identify the genre of the *Confessio* accurately and show how the structural elements thereof relate to one another.

Studies that have been made of the structure of the *Confessio* have tended to be merely descriptive; for example, Donald G. Schueler points out that the organization of the early books is geometric, whereas that of the later books is not, and he suggests that "Gower departed from this geometric kind of pattern ... [because] he had discovered there was no need for it" (17). Elizabeth D. Kirk observes that "both the *Confessio* and the *Canterbury Tales* are built concentrically, embedding simpler units in larger, formal ones, a kind of structure that Burrow calls 'encapsulation'" (114). Arno Esch, identifying the *Confessio* as "eine enzyklopädische Anlage" (208), argues that both the *Confessio* as a whole and the individual tales are constructed as a balance of such opposites as "sweet" and "useful." Although interesting and of some use to a beginning reader, such descriptions do not provide information that a reader cannot derive from a reading of the poem. Some modern critical approaches using linguistic and structuralist techniques of literary analysis that have been overlooked in relation to Gower although they have been profitably applied to numerous other medieval works can help us realize the breadth of scope of Gower's poetic art.

Chapter One

Reading the *Confessio Amantis*:
The Analogue of Dante's *Vita Nuova*

The standard perception of the structure of the *Confessio Amantis* is that it consists of a Prologue and eight books, which, with the exception of Book Seven, each examines one of the Seven Deadly Sins, encapsulating tales within a framework many critics perceive as "alien" (Tiller, 11). Because of this perception, many critics express puzzlement as to other aspects of the poem, especially why Gower included the Prologue, Book Seven--which is "a hiatus in the confession" (Schueler, "Some Comments" 21)---and the digression in Book Five that has been called "absolutely unnecessary" (Gower, vol. I: xx) by G. C. Macaulay, the most recent editor of the entire *Confessio*. Macaulay also criticizes the account in Book Five of religions other than Christianity, which he believes reaches "the highest pitch of grotesque absurdity when the Confessor occupies himself in demolishing the claim of Venus to be accounted a goddess" (Gower, vol. I: xx).

Some of the problems of interpreting and appreciating the *Confessio* properly in the twentieth century stem from the fact that it seems to be of no identifiable genre, although some critics have shown that aspects of it derive generically from Boethius (see Means, Peck, and, most recently, Cherniss, *Boethian Apocalypse*) and Ovid (see Hiscoe). We as readers find it difficult to understand how parts like the Prologue, the digression in Book Five, and Book Seven fit structurally into the whole. Medieval works were written in a world dominated by a high-context culture in which English and continental writers had common assumptions and wrote for audiences with similar expectations about the nature and importance of literature. Various aspects of the works written in this high-context culture illuminate one another in valuable ways. A work that helps us understand the genre of the *Confessio* as a whole and the structural relationship among its parts is Dante's *Vita Nuova*. Both poets write in a common tradition and owe much to sources like troubadour poetry and the *Roman de la Rose*, but their works are strikingly alike and yet different from others of the same period.[1] As a result, a comparison of the *Confessio* and the *Vita* helps us to understand Gower's structural signals.

One of the first structural signals that we need to interpret is the language of the *Confessio*. Although critics usually describe the *Confessio* as Gower's "English poem," in contrast to the *Vox Clamantis* (his "Latin poem") and the *Mirour d'Omme* (his "French poem"), he actually mingles "English verses, Latin verses, and Latin prose (Yeager, "oure englisshe" 41). Yeager points out that there are no other works "which mix languages and forms in exactly the same way" ("oure englisshe" 43) as the *Confessio*, but I would argue that the patterns can be described in terms of patterns of two languages (English and Latin) and two forms (prose and verse)--patterns reminiscent of the *Vita Nuova*, in which there are two languages (Italian and Latin) and a mixture of poetry and prose. Mark Musa argues that the *Vita* is original because it is "the first work of *fiction* including both prose and poetry" (ix) [italics mine] and that "the combination of the two [styles] represents a new literary genre in Italian literature" (132). The *Confessio* is a fictional work of the same genre, mixing prose and poetry, Latin and the vernacular in a way that is analogous to the mix which the *Vita* uses.

    The *Vita* also provides a partial analogue for the structure of the *Confessio* as a whole, and Gower seems to have merged various elements from his common medieval heritage to compose his work. It would have been logical for Gower to seek a model for his poem; although poetry was written in English (see Kean, I: 1), there was not "an exalted, *written*, literary tradition" (Coleman, 38) [italics mine]. In the fourteenth century, a serious poet writing in English "transferred the formula [of a literary work] to English, finding words to suit in the new language the structure and content of the old" (Coleman, 38). As a result, poets tried to discover "a *corresponding* rather than a wholly new language in the vernacular" (Coleman, "English Culture" 43) [italics Coleman's]. While composing the *Confessio*, Gower "transferred" the formula (that is, the genre) of works like the *Vita Nuova* to English, transforming it to accord with his own vision as he did so.

    The suggestion that it is helpful to view the *Vita* as a generic analogue for the *Confessio* seems especially plausible because one analogue is the type of work in which "prose commentaries on poetic texts ... [are] placed either in the margin or inside the text itself" (Yeager, "oure englisshe" 43), the type of work that has been shown to be the model for the *Vita* (see Singleton, 27). In the *Vita*, Dante depicts himself as a scribe who sometimes copies his text exactly while at other times giving the "sentenzia" (Singleton, 28) [italics deleted] of his original and providing a vernacular prose commentary on the poems that includes several key remarks in Latin.

    Gower provides a Latin prose commentary that similarly calls attention to the limitations of the poetic text. In the *Vita*, Dante's poems are written in the style of love poetry known as *dolce stil nuovo*. By incorporating the poems into a prose narrative that "explain[s] the occasion for the composition of each of the poems included" (Musa, x), however, Dante indicates his awareness of the limitations of the style, the need to do something new to catch the attention of his audience. Gower shares Dante's concern with style, and he says, "Forthi the Stile of my writinges/ Fro this day forth I thenke change" (I, 8-9), adopting a style appropriate to a discussion of love. In the *Confessio*, there is a complex relationship between the Latin prose and verse and the English verse, and in addition, Gower uses Rhyme Royal in lines 2217-2300 of Book Eight; the changes of form show Gower's concern with style. As Kurt O. Olsson reminds us, the *Confessio* is intended to be entertaining (see "Rhetoric" 196), and part of the entertainment involves the form in which it is written. Anthony E. Farnham argues that Gower wrote for an audience that would have enjoyed "the Latin marginalia and elegiac meters as an elegance well suited to moral wisdom" (165), adding that a modern reader "who assumes the marginal notes are mere summaries of the English verses will miss some of Gower's humor" (165). He points out (see 172) that the narrator claims to be "on of tho" (I, 62) who are lovers, while in the Latin, Gower says, "Hic quasi in persona aliorum, quos amor alligat, fingens se auctor esse Amantem, varias eorum passiones variis huius libri distinccionibus per singula scribere proponit" (vol. I: 37) [Here, as if in the role of the others, whom love binds, the author, representing himself to be Amans/a lover, proposes to write separately about each of these passions by means of the diverse divisions of his book]. Comparing the *Confessio* to the *Vita* reminds us that we need to read the Latin commentary in the *Confessio* as part of the work.

Amans, the protagonist of the *Confessio*, is a figure whose name means "the one loving" (Cowling, 64); in addition, Michael D. Cherniss notes that as "an exemplary figure" his name suggests a pun on "A-man" (*Boethian Apocalypse* 112). Amans resembles all the characters in medieval poetry who are defined by their state as lovers. In particular, however, Gower's Amans resembles the *Vita's* Dante the protagonist in some subtle ways; therefore, just as the knowledge that there is often "a relationship between Chaucer's self-portrait and Dante's" (Kellogg, 119) helps us appreciate Chaucer's artistry, the knowledge of a comparable relationship helps us to understand Gower's. One must differentiate between Dante the author and Dante the protagonist when reading the *Vita* (see Musa, 168), as we must between Chaucer the poet and Geoffrey the protagonist. We must do the same in the *Confessio*, in which Amans identifies himself as "John Gower" (VIII, 2321); Cherniss, indeed, suggests that the voice of "the poet of the Prologue and epilogue" differs from that of "Amans, the visionary-narrator" (*Boethian Apocalypse* 104). Musa calls the *Vita* "cruel" because of its "treatment of the human type represented by the protagonist" and its "condemnation of the vice of emotional self-indulgence" and "exposure of its destructive effects on a man's integrity" (171). At much greater length, Gower uses the device of the confession to expose Amans' self-indulgence in his love affair and his need to recapture his integrity. Samuel T. Cowling has argued that Amans, Genius, and the god and goddess of love "take part in an elaborate parody of the courtly lover's psychological experience" (63), a parody similar to that with which Dante the poet portrays Dante the protagonist.

Students of the *Vita* have tended to treat the work and the love it depicts seriously, seldom noting that Dante the author presents the protagonist "as a purely ridiculous figure" (Musa, 172) for comic purposes. Like the protagonist of the *Vita*, Amans is ridiculous. In Book Four, for example, Gower uses the marginalia to call attention to the fact that "non ... sic se habet veritas, set opinio Amantum" (vol. I: 340) [the following is not the truth, but the opinion of Amans]. As Macaulay observes, "the author dissociates himself personally from the extreme doctrines enunciated in the text" (Gower, vol. I: 506), and Gower says that the views of Amans lack veracity; as a result, Amans appears especially foolish. Characters within the works hold up the respective protagonists for our ridicule. Dante the author tells us that the ladies of Florence were at one time joking about him "con questa gentilissima" (Dante, 36) [with this most courteous one] after perceiving that his love makes him weak. Amans complains to Genius, "Mi wo to you is bot a game,/ That fielen noght of that I fiele" (VIII, 2152-53).

Just as the humor of the *Vita* has been overlooked, so has that of the *Confessio*, usually treated as "insistently didactic" (Peck, xxv); James Dean observes that nobody could consider Gower "a comic poet" (410). Farnham, however, calls the *Confessio* a "great joke" because of its "comic frame story of Amans, the would-be dirty old man, ... and Genius, the affable Confessor forever in a muddle over which God he serves" (172), and Frances McNeely Leonard notes that the *Confessio* includes comic passages (see 73). David W. Hiscoe has argued that readers must recognize "the organizing comic strategy" of the *Confessio* and the fact that it is, "not only a collection of medieval ethical lore, but also a *tour de force* of sustained humor" (368) [italics Hiscoe's]. Reading the *Confessio* as a work written in the same tradition as the *Vita* helps us understand the humor of the *Confessio*, a work which Gower himself says "stant betwene ernest and game" (VIII, 3109). The humor is to be expected in Gower's poetry if we consider what Burrow has shown to be characteristic of the Ricardian poets: "Matthew Arnold was right when he said that Chaucer lacked 'high poetic seriousness'. In Arnold's context, ... 'seriousness' implies speaking straight, not obliquely, to some great matter. Neither Chaucer nor his great contemporaries are often in this sense 'serious'. Their characteristic manner lies ... 'betwixt earnest and game'. This [involves an] oblique and often humorous approach to great matters--God, sin, death" (*Ricardian Poetry* 45). In addition to helping us understand the typically Ricardian humor of the *Confessio*, a comparison of the *Confessio* and the *Vita* suggests that Gower may have found in works of the genre of the *Vita* his inspiration both for the genre of his poem and for the humorous contents of his frame story.

When we perceive the similarity between the *Vita* and the *Confessio*, we are able to understand an important point about the structure of the *Confessio*: why Gower included both the Prologue and Book Seven and the digressions in Book Five. Gower included these sections for two reasons. First, without the Prologue, the *Confessio* would be structured around the Seven Deadly Sins rather than around love; since the Prologue speaks "of love, which is al the chief/ To kepe a regne out of meschief" (Pro., 149-50), it enables Gower to show that the subject of the *Confessio* is love.

The focus on love resembles that of other works. In the *Vita*, for example, Dante recounts how he came into contact with the love that thereafter governed his life: "Lo spirito de la vita ... disse queste parole: *Ecce deus fortior me, qui veniens dominabitur michi*" (19-20) [italics those of Chiappelli's edition of Dante's *Vita*] [The spirit of life spoke these words: "Behold a god stronger than I, who, when he comes, will rule over me"]. Gower, aware that he "may noght strecche up to the hevene/ ... [his] hand" (I, 1-2)--a passage that reminds a modern reader of what Dante did in the *Commedia*--chooses love as his subject, reminding us of the Dante who wrote the *Vita*: "I/ Woll wryte and schewe al openly/ How love and I togedre mette" (I, 83-85). Dante argues that "dal principio" (57) [from the beginning], vernacular poetic composition was intended "per dire d'amore" (57) [for speaking about love], and this statement shows us why a late medieval poet like Gower composed a poem about love "in oure englissh" (Pro., 23). Both poets are conscious of their audiences. Dante says that "lo primo che cominciò a dire sì come poeta volgare, si mosse però che volle fare intendere le sue parole a donna, a la quale era malagevole d'intendere li versi latini" (56) [the first person who began to speak as a vernacular poet was, however, moved by a desire to make his words intelligible to ladies who found Latin verses difficult to understand], and he addresses one poem to "donne ch'avete intelleto d'amore" (42) [italics deleted] [ladies who have knowledge of love]. Gower expresses a wish that "som man mai lyke" (Pro., 21) his writings, and his "decision to write in 'oure englissh'" indicates his understanding "of English (that 'middel weie') as the most appropriate medium in which to offer that 'lust' necessary to hold a reader's attention while the 'lore' sinks in" (Yeager, "oure englissh" 42-43). The use of English promotes the "game" of the *Confessio*, just as Dante's use of the vernacular promotes that of the *Vita*,[2] and it is therefore helpful to remember the *Vita* while reading the *Confessio*.

In addition to including the Prologue to emphasize that the *Confessio* is about love rather than sin, Gower may have included it and Book Seven as separate structural units in order to bring the number of sections of the *Confessio* to nine, an important number in medieval thought whose importance we can understand by reading the *Vita*. One of the noteworthy features of the *Vita* is its emphasis on the number nine; Dante says that Beatrice was "uno nove, cioè uno miracolo" (62) [a nine, that is, a miracle]. By structuring the *Confessio* as a nine-book work, Gower is able to re-examine the claim made by poets like Dante that human love and the beloved are miraculous, showing instead that they are examples of the partial goods that men must leave behind on their way to Heaven. His humor in this respect resembles that which Chauncey Wood sees in Boccaccio, who divides *Il Filostrato* into nine sections, taking the number used to represent Beatrice and using it "as the structural base for a poem claimed to be an inducement to seduction" (*Elements* 7).

Book Five, in which Gower discusses the fact that Venus and Cupid are not deities worthy of worship, is structurally at the center of the nine-section *Confessio*, but Gower's discussion of Venus and Cupid seems to undercut the fiction of the poem. The problems of interpreting Book Five resemble those of interpreting chapter twenty-five of the *Vita*, in which Dante seems to undercut the fictive level of his work by pointing out that "Amore non è per sé sì come sustanzia, ma è uno accidente in sustanzia" (56) [Love does not exist in itself as a substance, but it exists as an accident in a substance]. "Amore" [Love] is, however, an ambiguous term in the *Vita*, in which love appears in two forms, "the Greater" and "the Lesser Aspect" (Musa, 120). Musa points out that "the figure of love capable of representing either the Greater or the Lesser Aspect, appears for the first time in Chapter III ..., shifting from the Greater to the Lesser, back to the Greater Aspect again" (120). Charles S. Singleton has argued that the *Vita* is "a gradual disclosure of the true nature of love" (56) and that chapter twenty-five marks the transition from earthly love, *amor*, to heavenly love, *caritas*,[3] or, using Musa's terms, from the Lesser Aspect to the Greater. In the *Confessio*, Gower makes the same transition, and I should like to suggest that he placed Book Five at the center of his work to predispose us to accept Amans' rejection of earthly love for heavenly at the end of the poem. Because it shows us the falsity of earthly love and its deities, Book Five marks the transition from *amor* to *caritas*, a fact we appreciate by comparison to chapter twenty-five of the *Vita*.

In both the *Vita* and the *Confessio*, the protagonists meet the god of love. A meeting between a lover who is the narrator of a medieval poem, especially a dream vision, and the god of love is a commonplace of medieval poems like the *Roman de la Rose* because the figure "unites the erotic pagan world with the Christian tradition" (Kiser, 22) and makes it possible for poets to treat secular love by using religious symbolism. However, Dante and Gower use the god of love as the inverse of the usual allegorical symbol, exploring secular love symbolically to determine the meaning of religious love.

Because the *Confessio*'s use of the god of love is closer to that of the *Vita* than to that of other works, including the *Roman* and the *Legend of Good Women*, it is useful to compare the two gods as poetic figures. In a vision, the god tells Dante the protagonist, "Ego dominus tuus" (22) [italics deleted] [I am your lord]. Likewise, in the *Confessio*, the god of love is Amans' lord, throwing through his "herte rote" (I, 145) a "firy Dart" (I, 144) which recalls the fact that the god appeared to Dante the protagonist in "una nebula di colore di fuoco" (22) [a cloud the color of fire] holding "una cosa la quale ardesse tutta" (22) [a thing that was all burning]. The fire represents sexual passion; Amans addresses the god as "Cupide, god of loves lawe,/ That with thi Dart brennende hast set afyre/ Min herte" (VIII, 2287-89). In neither the *Vita* nor the *Confessio* is the god of love present during the entire work. In the *Vita*, he does not appear in the second half of the work, and his nonappearance represents "nothing less than a deliberate removal" (Singleton, 74) which makes way for "a conception of love held by saints and mystics" (Singleton, 60). By the removal, Dante prepares us for the protagonist's renunciation of human, sexual love in favor of the love of God. In the *Confessio*, the god of love "forth wente" (I, 143) after piercing Amans' heart, and he does not reappear until the end of the poem, at which time "he pulleth oute" (VIII, 2800) the "fyri Lancegay" (VIII, 2798), an image that represents Amans' renunciation of sexual love. Thereafter, the "blinde god" (VIII, 2794) disappears once more.

Dante the protagonist and Amans serve the god of love because, like all medieval lovers, each is what Alain Renoir calls a "frustrated lover" who desires a "reluctant mistress" ("Inept Lover" 183), a beautiful but unresponsive lady. The *Vita* and the *Confessio* are similar, however, in their depiction of this *topos*, portraying--to borrow Musa's statement about the *Vita*--"the (tender) foolishness of the lover [which] is intensified by contrast with the (icy) perfection of the Belovèd" (173), a perfection that is more than human. In the *Vita*, Dante describes Beatrice with phrases like "angiola giovanissima" (20) [the youngest of the angels], applying to her the words of Homer, "Ella non parea figliuola d'uomo mortale, ma di deo" (20) [She did not seem to be the daughter of a mortal man, but of a god]. His judgment is backed by that of the Florentines, who say of Beatrice, "Questa non è femmina, anzi è uno de li bellisiimi angeli del cielo" (58) [This is not a woman; on the contrary, she is one of the most beautiful angels of Heaven], calling her "una maraviglia" (58) [a marvel].

Dante eliminates almost all physical details, with the result that Beatrice "does not have a face in the prose narrative of the *Vita*" (Musa, 103) but appears in "the red of *caritas*, [or] the white of purity" (Musa, 103) [italics Musa's]. By this type of presentation, Dante makes Beatrice the *donna angelicata* figure familiar from lyric poetry. Amans neither describes nor names his lady, but he emphasizes "hire beaute" (II, 2580) and says that he enjoys hearing people say "how that my ladi berth the pris,/ How sche is fair, how sche is wis,/ How sche is wommanlich of chiere" (I, 2755-57). Dante says that Beatrice had come "in tanta grazia de le genti, che quando passava per via, le persone correano per vedere lei" (58) [into so much favor among the people that, when she walked along the street, people ran to see her], although she was always "coronata e vestita d'umilitade" (58) [crowned and clothed with humility]. Like Beatrice, Amans' Lady preserves "hire honour ate alle tide" (II, 59) and is characterized by "gentilesse" (III, 488). She, however, is not an angel, although Amans says that the sight of her is "of Paradis the moste joie" (VI, 207). Instead, she is a real woman who can be courted and escorted to "masse" (IV, 1133) by her lover.

Dante's love is pure, and "lo fine del ... amore" (41) [the end of his love] originally lies in "lo saluto" (41) [the greeting] of Beatrice. Like Dante the protagonist, Amans is glad when "hire like ywiss/ To speke a goodli word" (III, 98-99). After Beatrice refuses to greet him, Dante finds the purpose of love in writing poetry that praises her; as he says, his purpose lies "in quelle parole che lodano la donna" (41) [in those words that praise the lady]. Amans is also pleased with words that praise his lady: "Whanne I may hiere sain/ Tidinges of my ladi hele,/ Althogh I may noght with hire dele,/ Yit am I wonder glad of that" (I, 2760-63).

Amans has a more practical aim than does Dante, because he wishes to "welden" (II, 2411, and V, 77) his lady at his own "wille" (II, 2411, and V, 77), and "welden" means "to wield a woman, that is, to possess, enjoy, or swive a mistress" (Donaldson, 9); like Boccaccio, Gower wittily adapts imagery about an idealized lady to a poem about seduction. Amans dreams that he "al one with hire mete/ And that Danger is left behinde" (IV, 2902-3) so that he is able to make love to her. Even the poems that Amans writes have the practical purpose of seduction, and he expresses his concern that he "ferde ... noght the bet" (I, 2735) for having written them. Although Amans has composed "rondeal, balade and virelai/ For hire" (I, 2727-28) as well as "caroles" (I, 2730) that he wishes to sing to his lady, "sche saide it was noght for hir sake,/ And liste noght ... [his] songes hiere/ Ne witen what the wordes were" (I, 2740-42). The episode is reminiscent of the fact that when Dante pretends to be in love with the second screen-lady, Beatrice hears "soverchievole voce" (29) [exaggerated rumors] that depict Dante as "infamasse viziosamente" (29) [a dreadful person] so that he cannot persuade her that he loves her. Amans depicts himself as a "dreadful person," saying of women other than his lady, "I have tasted/ In many a place as I have go,/ And yit love I nevere on of tho,/ Bot forto drive forth the dai" (V, 7792-95).

Dante says that from the time that he first saw Beatrice, "Amore segnoreggiò" (20) [Love governed] his "anima" (20) [soul], and his love lasts even after her death. Amans similarly swears, "for o lokinge of hire yë/ Min hole herte til I dye/ With al that evere I may and can/ Sche hath me wonne to hire man" (V, 4493-96), and he avers, "for god wot, thogh I nevere scholde/ Sen hir with yhe after this day,/ Yit stant it so that I ne may/ Hir love out of my brest remue" (I, 1324-27). He makes his vows for a practical purpose, because, like a typical courtly lover, he assumes that since she is loved, "good reson wolde/ That sche somdel rewarde scholde" (V, 4497-98). When he learns that his sexual love cannot prosper because he is old and Venus bids him "go ther vertu moral duelleth" (VIII, 2925), he forgets his lady and thinks and speaks of God.

Dante's love is depicted with humorous seriousness. He says that when Beatrice refused to greet him, he was overcome "tanto dolore" (30) [with great grief], and when he found himself unexpectedly in her company, his "spiriti" (36) [spirits] were "distrutti ... per la forza che Amore prese veggendosi in tanta propinquitate a la gentilissima donna" (36) [destroyed by the force which Love acquired by such propinquity to the most courteous lady]. People divine his secret when it becomes apparent that he is unable even to "sostenere la sua presenza" (41) [bear her presence].

In the *Confessio*, in contrast, Amans, who warns his audience that he pursues his love affair "evere in ernest and in game" (IV, 50), merely plays at being the lover who cannot endure his lady's company. He says that he is "of hire adrad" (IV, 572) and that he is "so ferful" (IV, 360) that he "dar noght speke" (IV, 360) to her of his purpose. After hearing the story of Ulysses, he says, "Whanne I may my lady hiere,/ Mi wit with that hath lost his Stiere:/ I do noght as Uluxes dede,/ But falle anon upon the stede,/ Wher as I se my lady stonde" (I, 559-63). The source of his fear and diffidence is the fact that his lady refuses to become his mistress: "Bot rathere I am *ofte adrad*/ For sorwe that sche seith me nay" (I, 2748-49) [italics mine]. In contrast to the protagonist of the *Vita*, Amans spends as much time as possible with his lady. In the evening, when "sche bidt" (IV, 2802) him leave her, he swears that "it is even liht" (IV, 2804) in order to stay longer. However, when he must at last "fro hire wende" (IV, 2807) even though he "loth is forto take his leve" (IV, 2815), he bids her farewell, sometimes making an excuse to return: "If that I dore,/ Er I come fulli to the Dore,/ I torne ayein and feigne a thing,/ As thogh I hadde lost a Ring/ Or somwhat elles, for I wolde/ Kisse hire eftsones, if I scholde,/ Bot selden is that I so spede./ And whanne I se that I mot nede/ Departen, I departe" (IV, 2825-33). Like Dante, Gower treats human love with humorous irony. As Farnham points out, however, part of the humor of the *Confessio* derives from the fact that Amans is "frustrated and bewildered by an emotional commitment of embarrassing purity" (172). Analogous purity never embarrasses Dante but leads him eventually to his vision of God at the end of the *Paradiso*.

The problem with human, sexual love for medieval poets like Dante and Gower is that it is a love that is often sinful and must be recanted by the lover if he is to reach Heaven. As Singleton points out, "there is no room and no authority for a troubadour God of Love in the universe of Christian love" (75), so that the lover must eventually recant his love for his lady. Singleton argues that Dante's love for Beatrice, which changes from an earthly to a heavenly love, differs from the loves expressed in other medieval works: "A troubadour's love would have seen only Beatrice, a saint's love would have sought only God" (77). The god of love disappears from the *Vita* in the middle, and he is replaced by Beatrice, who "holds a medial position, not only in the downward path of love from God to man but in the upward and returning path of love from man to God as well" (Singleton, 77). As a result, although the *Vita* eventually recants earthly love, it keeps "love of woman to the very end" (Singleton, 77), ultimately making the beloved lady the transcendent representative of God's love.

In the *Confessio*, there is a more complicated pattern than a transition from the god of love to the beloved who is the intermediary between God and man. Part of the difference is that Gower, although later than Dante, is closer to the troubadours in his point of view (see Audiau, 113). Therefore, he moves from the troubadour love devoted to the lady to the love of God. Amans meets "the kyng of love and qweene bothe" (I, 139) rather than merely the god, and when the god of love ceases to be his master, the "qweene" remains. Venus and her priest Genius play the guiding role that the god of love plays in the first half of the *Vita*, a fact to which Amans calls attention by addressing Venus in French as "Ma dame" (I, 168) [my lady] and Genius in Latin as "Dominus" (I, 215) [lord], terms that recall the god's statement in the *Vita*, "Ego dominus tuus" (22) [italics deleted] [I am your lord]. The god addresses the protagonist of the *Vita* as "Fili mi" (30) [italics deleted] [my son], but it is Venus who calls Amans "Sone" (I, 154) and Genius who addresses him as "Mi Sone" (I, 206, for example). When the god of love disappears from the *Vita*, Beatrice remains as Dante the protagonist's guide. In the *Confessio*, in contrast, when the god "pulleth oute" (VIII, 2800) the "fyri Lancegay" (VIII, 2798) with which he had pierced Amans' heart in Book One and then disappears so that Amans "not where he becam" (VIII, 2802), it is Venus rather than Amans' lady who is Amans' guide and teaches him that he must recant earthly love. With an "oignement" (VIII, 2817), she anoints Amans' "wounded herte" (VIII, 2818), "temples" (VIII, 2819), and "Reins" (VIII, 2819), and she shows him "a wonder Mirour" (VIII, 2821) in which he beholds his "Elde" (VIII, 2828) so that he comes to acknowledge that he is in "the Wynter [that] wol no Somer knowe" (VIII, 2853). Giving him "a Peire of Bedes blak as Sable" (VIII, 2904) around which is written "Por reposer" (VIII, 2907) [italics deleted] [in order to rest], she bids him go "ther vertu moral duelleth" (VIII, 2925) and "preie hierafter for the pes" (VIII, 2913).

In the scene in Book Eight, Venus changes from the goddess of human, sexual love who was rejected in Book Five to a representative of heavenly love. She is the "queene" (VIII, 2899) to whom Amans/Gower kneels, resembling the Virgin Mary, the true female intermediary between

God and man in the Middle Ages. The merger of Venus and Mary is used by Chaucer as well as Gower, and F. N. Robinson observes that Chaucer speaks to Venus in the proem to Book III of *Troilus and Criseyde* in a way that echoes words conventionally "addressed to the Virgin" (Chaucer, 823). In Book Eight of the *Confessio*, the similarity between Venus and Mary is enhanced by the fact that Venus "mai the hertes bynde/ In loves cause and ek unbinde" (VIII, 2811-12), a power like that of the female persona of the Church.

When Venus leaves Amans and, "enclosid in a sterred sky" (VIII, 2942), is "take in to hire place above" (VIII, 2944)--lines that emphasize her resemblance to Mary--Gower turns to a consideration of heavenly love. In a Latin prose gloss near the end of the poem, he states, "Concludit enim quod omnis amoris delectacio extra caritatem nichil est. Qui autem manet in caritate, in deo manet" (vol. II: 475) [Indeed, this {the poem} argues that the delight of all love except *caritas* is nothing. But he who remains in *caritas*, remains in God]. This gloss makes the transition from *amor* to *caritas* an explicit part of the *Confessio*. Gower, who promises "nomore of love make,/ Which many an herte hath overtake" (VIII, 3143-44), is aware that one must fully renounce earthly love and turn to *caritas*:

> Bot thilke love which that is
> Withinne a mannes herte affermed,
> And stant of charite confermed,
> Such love is goodly forto have,
> Such love mai the bodi save,
> Such love mai the soul amende,
> The hyhe god such love ous sende
> Forthwith the remenant of grace;
> So that above in thilke place
> Wher resteth love and alle pes,
> Oure joie mai ben endeles.
> (VIII, 3162-72)

Singleton argues that there is an image at the beginning of the *Vita* which provides a governing metaphor for the work, that of the Book of Memory (see 25). Although Gower does not use a similar term, the metaphor helps us to appreciate the *Confessio*, which purports to depict his memory of an actual experience,[4] his confession to Genius complete with the stories Genius told him. Gower says he wrote the *Confessio* so that the reader "schal drawe into remembrance/ The fortune of this worldes chance" (Pro., 69-70), and when he speaks of temporal rulers, he says, "If I schal drawe in to my mynde/ The tyme passed" (Pro., 93-94). Although "betwen ernest and game" (Pro., 462), such statements show clearly that the

Confessio is a Book of Memory analogous to the earlier Book of Memory of the same genre. The point of Gower's Book of Memory becomes clear at the end of the *Confessio*, when Venus shows Amans his face in a mirror and he realizes that he is old. He says, "thanne into my remembrance/ I drowh myn olde daies passed" (VIII, 2834-35), recalling his life and turning from earthly love to the saving love of God. Dante recants his love, but the *Vita* "represents the most original form of recantation in medieval literature" because it "takes the form of a reenactment, from a new perspective, of the sin recanted" (Musa, 174). The *Confessio* similarly re-enacts the details of Amans' love before Amans/Gower recants it. It, however, re-enacts much more than does the *Vita*: not just the story of one man's love, but the stories of all human loves, sins, and griefs, re-enacted through the framed stories narrated.

When we compare the *Confessio* to the *Vita*, we can understand Gower's adaptation of one of the set-pieces of love poetry, the vision given the protagonist by the god of love who is the "dominus" [lord] of the lover. Gower's adaptation of this episode both suggests his dependence on the tradition and shows his differences therefrom. Musa argues that in the *Vita*, the visionary experience is more important than waking life because in his vision, "the protagonist is offered glimpses of eternity" (106). Like Dante the protagonist, Amans receives "glimpses of eternity," because he sees the lovers' paradise from which he is excluded because of his age; in the *Vita*, Dante was excluded from his personal paradise first when Beatrice refused him "lo suo dolcissimo salutare" (29) [her most sweet greeting] and then upon her death. In the *Vita*, the first "maravigliosa visione" (21) [marvelous vision] is of "una figura d'uno segnore di pauroso aspetto" (22) [a figure of a lord of frightening appearance]. Amans also sees a frightening god, who "with yhen wrothe/ His chiere aweiward from ... [Amans] caste" (I, 140-41). Singleton argues that the three visions of the *Vita* "foretell the death of Beatrice" (15); I believe that they also foretell the transfiguration of the protagonist's earthly love for her into *caritas*.

Gower places the lover's crucial vision, not at the beginning, but at the end of the work, and it occurs after Amans has prayed, "Do that wounde be withdrawe,/ Or yif me Salve such as I desire" (VIII, 2289-90). Amans says that "in Avision/ ... [he] hadde a revelacion" (VIII, 2805-6), given to him when he feels like "a man [who] the blase of fyr/ With water quencheth" (VIII, 2444-45); he is caught by "a cold" (VIII, 2446) and falls down "swoune" (VIII, 2449). Dante the protagonist sees the god of love bearing his beloved, "la donna de la salute" (22) [the lady of the greeting]. Although Amans sees "Cupide with his bowe bent" (VIII, 2453), he sees, not his beloved, but "gentil folk that whilom were/ Lovers" (VIII, 2457-58), excluding himself. In the *Confessio*, the vision foreshadows only the death of earthly love, not the death of the beloved lady. By placing the crucial vision given the lover at the end, Gower makes the recantation of earthly love clearer than it is in the *Vita*. "Amans is liberated" (Olsson, "Rhetoric" 197) by his vision, whereas Dante is only liberated after years of reflection. By the placement of the vision, Gower contradicts the point of view expressed by Dante, who suggests that it is specifically the love of a lady that leads man to God while sharing with other medieval love poets the acknowledgement that earthly love must at some point be recanted. Gower presents the troubadour view that the love of a lady is a partial good that must be left behind on the road to Heaven.

Musa argues that Dante makes the god of love represent both aspects of love, *amor* and *caritas*, in order to explore "the paradoxical nature of love" (124), a theme that Gower also explores.[5] Gower's Venus represents both aspects of love, because it is she who gives Amans a rosary at the end of the poem. Recent critics have shown that love is more complex in the *Confessio* than early critics realized, deliberately ambiguous and hard to understand. J. A. W. Bennett, for example, argues that "'honeste love' in wedlock, *caritas* in the commonwealth, are wholly compatible ideals, and it is Gower's distinctive achievement to have harmonized them in a single poem" (121) [italics Bennett's]. Gower says, "who that al of wisdom writ/ It dulleth ofte a mannes wit" (Pro., 13-14), and he vows therefore that he "wolde go the middle weie/ And wryte a bok between the tweie,/ Somwhat of lust, somwhat of lore" (Pro., 17-19). At the end of the poem, he reasserts his interest in "lust" and "lore," saying that he "undirtok/ In englesch forto make a book/ Which stant betwene ernest and game" (VIII, 3107-9).

Many critics have all but ignored the "game" of the *Confessio*, arguing, as Russell A. Peck does, that the *Confessio* deals with Gower's "ideas on man's moral obligations" (xxiii). I should like to suggest that we do a disservice to the "lore" of the *Confessio* unless we understand the "game" of the poem, including its structure. Furthermore, understanding that the structure of the *Confessio* resembles that of the *Vita Nuova* helps us to appreciate the "game." In contrast to Dante, Gower has a mellow view of the world, one in which there is room for much more than love alone. The story of Amans frames stories that make comparisons between "ethical conduct in affairs of the heart and ethical conduct in general" (Weinberg, 11), stories that show that Gower finds room for all the world, viewed from the charitable perspective of one who has passed from earthly to heavenly love. Unlike the *Vita*, the *Confessio* is more than a tribute to youthful love; but to read it properly, we must pay close attention to its structure. If we grant the assumption of this chapter, that the *Confessio* resembles the *Vita*, we realize that the Prologue, Book Five, and Book Seven play essential roles in its structure. We then have pragmatic reasons for assuming that the remainder of the *Confessio* has a careful and precise structure rather than consisting merely of a random series of tales loosely attached to the Seven Deadly Sins.

Chapter Two

The Grammar of the *Confessio Amantis*

Scholars who have studied the *Confessio Amantis* have usually been concerned only with material in the frame story or with individual encapsulated narratives rather than with the work as a whole.[1] This concern resembles that which medievalists have shown in regard to authors like Chaucer and Boccaccio, both of whom present critical problems to the modern reader similar to those presented by Gower, because all retell traditional stories. Tzvetan Todorov has observed that "Boccacce a lui-même indiqué la voie à suivre dans la conclusion du livre: il n'a pas INVENTÉ ces histoires, dit-il, mais il les a ÉCRITES. C'est, en effet, dans l'écriture que se crée l'unité; les motifs que l'étude du folklore nous fait connaître sont transformés par l'écriture boccaccienne" (12) [italics Todorov's]. A similar statement could be made about the *Confessio Amantis*. In his *Grammaire du Décaméron*, Todorov presents a corrective balance to the critical emphasis on "l'analyse réelle du texte" (16), stating his purpose: "Les nouvelles particulières que nous trouvons dans le *Décaméron* ne seront pas considérées pour elles-mêmes, mais en vue de l'analyse de la narration qui est une entité abstraite. Chaque nouvelle particulière n'est que la manifestation d'une structure abstraite, une réalisation qui était contenue à l'état latent dans une combinatoire des possibles" (17). By his study, he provides a model for the study of other works that consist of stories drawn from various sources encapsulated in a frame narrative, although the model must naturally be adjusted to meet the needs of the work in question.

As Susan Wittig points out, there are problems in the approach to medieval literature taken by scholars like Todorov, especially a critical tendency to "apply models designed for sentence analysis directly to larger and less clearly defined units of narrative" (3) with the result that the model distorts the narrative. Nevertheless, if care be taken, the syntactical models can be adapted in a useful way to discuss larger units of narrative. Wittig's aim--to develop a model that is "derived inductively from the texts themselves" (4)--is the aim of the present study.[2]

One of the earliest and most profitable models, which is still of use in the study of medieval literature, is Eugene Dorfman's *The Narreme in the Medieval Romance Epic: An Introduction to Narrative Structures*; Boitani has used Dorfman's model to explain the structure of the tale of Pope Boniface (see *English Medieval Narratives* 128). Dorfman presents a theory about "the functional analysis of literary structures into constituent units, *narremes*, parallel with the phonemes and morphemes of linguistic analysis" (ix) [italics Dorfman's]. He argues that "the structure of a narrative may thus be analyzed in two ways: as a larger chain, containing all the incidents, central and marginal, that form the complete story; and as a much smaller chain of functionally central incidents, linked to each other in an organic relationship. By reason of their special function as core incidents in the structure of the narrative, these central units will be called *narremes*" (5) [italics Dorfman's]. The narremes of the *Confessio* differ, of course, from those of the Romance epic, but the term is a useful one, and I will adopt it in this chapter.

Another useful application to a medieval literary work of a technique developed for the analysis of sentences was made by Howard, who points out that "a stream of spoken discourse is a series of ... units put together by ... rules. One kind of unit is *juncture*--the 'pauses' which divide one sentence, phrase, or word from another, but which join them too, and in such a way as to make relationships clear. The term is useful if we are to talk about a literary structure whose units are tales. We need to look for the kinds of junctures between the tales: they seem to be 'pauses' or gaps or starting points, but if there is structure at all they are points where units are *related*" (211) [italics Howard's]. Howard argues that junctures of importance for the structure of the *Canterbury Tales* are found at three points, "where there is (1) a new teller or tale, (2) a new series of tales, or (3) a new theme" (211).

The linguistic idea of juncture helps us to appreciate the care with which Gower has built the structure of the *Confessio*. On the highest narrative level of the *Confessio*, the junctures are the separations between the nine sections of the poem, the Prologue and the eight books. Schueler notes that at the end of Book Six, "the Lover himself asks for a respite in order to learn how Alexander the Great was taught by Aristotle" (21), a passage which introduces the apparent digression that is Book Seven. I believe that Gower uses this device to call attention to the importance of juncture in the *Confessio*.

On the second highest narrative level of the *Confessio*, juncture occurs when a new speaker--Amans, Genius, Venus, or the god of Love--begins to speak, a kind of juncture analogous to that in the *Canterbury Tales* where a new teller is introduced or a new tale begins. Within the books, junctures also occur at points which Gower indicates by Latin verses that subdivide each book. Within speeches by Genius, juncture occurs between stories Genius tells to illustrate a particular point. The last type of juncture occasionally makes it hard to determine exactly how many narratives are encapsulated in the *Confessio*, a problem related to another problem with the encapsulated narratives: some traditional stories are found in several books. Portions of the story of Ulysses, for example, are found in Books One, Four, Five, and Six, in each case as an exemplum of a different sin, and the last episode concludes with his death.[3] In addition, some tales are embedded in others as the tale of Alceste (VII, 1917-43) is embedded in the tale of the King, Wine, Woman, and Truth (VII, 1811-1975). In order to appreciate Gower's structural method, one needs to consider the junctures at particular points rather than the stories as narrative units.

On the smallest level of structure in the *Confessio*, there is the structure of individual tales. There have been many excellent studies of individual tales, including of the structure thereof. Peter Goodall, for example, studies the tale of Appolinus of Tyre in Book Eight, pointing out that the most important obstacle to understanding it is structural: "First, there is the internal problem--the coherence of an episodic narrative--and, second, the external problems--what structural or thematic relationship does the tale bear to the rest of Book VIII, and then, to the rest of the *Confessio Amantis*?" (243). Arguing that Gower's work is not as loose structurally as is often claimed, Goodall analyzes the fact that there is "within the story a network of parallel scenes and contrasting situations and characters" (243). He views the relationship of the tale to the remainder of the *Confessio* as thematic through "the issue of Providence" (248) and the relationship to the rest of Book Eight as being also thematic because both the tale of Appolinus and the frame material deal with Fortune.

Even so fine a study as that of Goodall, which illuminates puzzling details in the tale of Appolinus and shows its structural excellence, concentrates too much on the smallest narrative level of the *Confessio* and does a disservice to our impression of the whole by suggesting that the links between the sections are purely thematic. In chapter five, I argue that to interpret the tale of Appolinus correctly, one must perceive the structural use therein of elements derived from an originally oral-formulaic tradition. At this point, I should like to examine the narremes and junctures of the larger structural units of the *Confessio* like those of Book Eight because so doing clears up many puzzling interpretative details. Book Eight, for example, has often been criticized; as Goodall points out, to many readers the conclusion seems anti-climactic (see 252). The fact that it is often called the Epilogue implies that readers view it as standing outside the structure of the *Confessio* in the same way as the Prologue seems to. Nevertheless, as Hans-Jürgen Diller shows, the concluding sections do not "form structural units within the text" (46), and the fact that Gower does not make the so-called Epilogue a separate structural unit as he makes the Prologue indicates that it is an integral part of the structure of Book Eight. Thematically, Book Eight is a single unit; as Peck suggests, it deals with "the rediscovery of right relationships" (161), and I would argue that the structure reinforces the thematic issues.

Part of the problem with the interpretation of Book Eight as a single structural unit lies in the fact that its main division is between the stories of Appolinus and of Amans, and critics seem to feel that because the story of

Amans purports to be biographical and Amans identifies himself as "John Gower" (VIII, 2321), there is a difference between the encapsulated narratives and the story of Amans. If, as I argued in chapter one, we acknowledge that there is a difference between Gower the author and Amans the protagonist--a difference most scholars grant exists between Chaucer the poet and Geoffrey the protagonist of the poems and between Dante the poet and Dante the protagonist--then we realize that Appolinus and Amans are equally fictitious characters in the *Confessio*.

The stories of Appolinus and Amans are what Dorfman calls "core incidents in the structure of the narrative" (5)--in this case, the narrative of Book Eight--and they may accordingly be identified as narremes within the book. The other encapsulated stories narrated in Book Eight by Genius-- the origin of mankind, the laws of marriage, the stories of Caligula, Amon, and Lot and his daughters, and the prayers for England and meditation on the state of the land which conclude the poem--are what Dorfman calls "marginal incidents" (6), necessary to the "linear progression" (6) of the book and to the characterization of the loquacious Genius but not part of "the *superstructure* of the story" (Dorfman, 6) [italics Dorfman's]. Dorfman's "test of a narreme is that it be the organic consequence of the preceding narreme and the effective cause of the following one" (6-7), a test that can be applied to the alternation between the *exempla* told by Genius and the story of Amans in each book of the *Confessio*.

In Book Eight, Gower calls attention to the two narremes in part because there are only two of them and in part because he shifts the point of view from "dialogue and debate between Genius and Amans" to "first person narration" (Peck, 174). The switch calls attention to these two narremes, and the use of the first-person point of view emphasizes that "the final narreme ... is the natural outcome of what has preceded" (Dorfman, 6) because the first person is especially appropriate for the summation of the poem. Furthermore, the final narreme provides a contrast to the initial narreme in Book One: Amans' identification of himself as John Gower "marks a new beginning" (Peck, 176) that shows that Amans is learning to understand himself, providing a contrast to the "Caitif that lith hiere" (I, 161) of Book One.

Dorfman suggests that the importance of narremes lies "in the possibilities of narremic opposition" (219) to develop a story; in the *Confessio*, the opposition lies in the alternation between the portions of dialogue attributed to Amans and those attributed to other characters. This alternation works structurally to permit Gower to develop the *Confessio* as a unified whole. Peck has suggested that the result of the switch to the first-person point of view is that the poem becomes internalized and the dialogue seems "to be going on within an Amans of past time" (174). The final narreme of the poem thus provides opposition both to the story of

Appolinus and to the remainder of the poem. Critics argue about the exact relationship between the stories of Appolinus and Amans; Peck views each as a story of "happy homecoming" (172), that of Appolinus from exile and that of Amans from "spiritual exile" (172), and Patrick J. Gallacher argues that the story of Appolinus "concerns the hardships of even rightly ordered human love, [and] is meant to help Amans make a transition to divine love" (144). Nevertheless, the structure of the poem shows that there is a relationship and that the conclusion is not an anti-climactic afterthought. In addition, it clearly functions in binary opposition to the remainder of the *Confessio* because it provides the answer to the problem of unsuccessful love that Amans has at the beginning of Book One, set within the framework of love announced by the Prologue.

The Prologue stands outside the narremic structure of the *Confessio* and serves to introduce the subject matter of the entire poem. Book One contains what Dorfman calls "the initial narreme, which serves as the necessary foundation for what is to follow" (6), Amans' waking vision that begins during a walk "in the Monthe of Maii,/ Whan every brid hath chose his make" (I, 100-1). In the vision, he sees "the kyng of love and qweene bothe" (I, 139) and receives the command that he confess to Genius. Once Genius "was redy there and sette him doun" (I, 201) to hear Amans' confession, the structure of the remainder of the poem is determined: the *Confessio* is partly modelled on confessional manuals (see Utley, Owst, and Braswell), a genre whose purpose is "to elicit a verbal response" (Gallacher, 1). As a result of "general agreement regarding the doctrine of penance in all its variety--from the attitudes of confessors and their functions in delineating for the penitent the cardinal sins and their contraries to the penitent's own responsibilities for contrition and amendment" (Kinneavy, 156)--the audience would expect the *Confessio* to be organized as a dialogue between Genius and Amans. Gower calls attention to the confessional nature of the dialogue with a Latin gloss in Book One, "Opponit Confessor. Respondet Amans" (vol. I: 51) [The Confessor interposes. Amans replies], thereby reinforcing our expectations about the nature of the poem. As Schueler points out, a dialogue depends "for its structural integrity on the naturalness ... with which it flows along" (17), and Gower deliberately presents a naturalistic dialogue. The initial narreme of the *Confessio* therefore establishes the narremic pattern of the whole, because the narremes of each book, like those of Book Eight, are based on the juncture between the *exempla* given by Genius and the application to the life of Amans.

Because the *Confessio* is in part based on confessional manuals, the audience would also expect Genius to introduce the Seven Deadly Sins in a systematic way, as he does in those books which are structured around Amans' sins against love. The juncture between the books is therefore important because it signals the systematic introduction of the Sins found in actual confession. This expectation is deliberately undermined by Book Seven, which Macaulay considers an unjustifiable "deliberate departure from the general plan" (Gower, vol. I: xix) of the *Confessio* but which is important to understand if we wish to understand the structure of the *Confessio*. As I argued in chapter one, the inclusion of Book Seven is important to understand if we wish to understand the structure of the *Confessio*: it helps minimize the focus of the *Confessio* on sin. In addition, when we examine its relationship to the narremic pattern of the *Confessio*, we see that the junctures between it and Books Six and Eight resemble those between all the books of the *Confessio* except that between Books Five and Six. At the end of Book Five, Amans says, "Toward mi schrifte as it belongeth,/ To wite of othre pointz me longeth;/ Wherof that ye me wolden teche/ With al myn herte I you beseche" (V, 7841-44), and Genius begins Book Six with an exposition of "the grete Senne original" (VI, 1), gluttony. As a result, the division between Books Five and Six is along the pattern of the dialogue and separates two narremes, Amans' question and Genius' reply. This juncture emphasizes that Book Five is an especially important structural unit in the *Confessio*; as I have argued in chapter one, it is also thematically important because it prepares us for the movement from *amor* to *caritas* at the conclusion of the *Confessio*.

In the rest of the poem, the juncture between books is not identical with that between narremes but occurs in the middle of speeches by Genius. At the end of Book One, Genius says that he intends to turn from stories "touchende of Prides fare" (I, 3435) to those "touchende Envie" (I, 3441), and at the beginning of Book Two, he says, "Now after Pride the secounde/ Ther is" (II, 1-2), identifying it as "that vice [that] is cleped hot Envie" (I, 10). At the end of Book Two, he promises to tell "which vice stant next after this" (II, 3527), identifying it at the beginning of Book Three as "a vice forein fro the lawe" (III, 5) which "cleped is the cruel Ire" (III, 15). At the end of Book Three, he promises to teach "the pointz of Slowthe" (III, 2774), beginning Book Four with "the ferste point of Slowthe ...,/ Lachesce" (III, 3-4). At the end of Book Four, he speaks of "the forme bothe and the matiere" (IV, 3712) of the next vice, Avarice, and at the beginning of Book Five, he contrasts the golden age "whan the hyhe god began/ This world" (V, 1-2) to the world under the rule of Avarice. At the end of Book Seven, he speaks of "love which is unavised" (VII, 5433), turning at the beginning of Book Eight to the subject of the Creation and Fall of Lucifer, whose "dedly Pride" (VIII, 23) brought about all the other sins, including lechery. The juncture between Books Six and Seven is identical to that between most of the other books, a division between types of subject matter only. Amans asks about the education of Alexander the Great, and Genius answers, "For thogh I be noght al cunnynge/ Upon the forme of this wrytynge,/ Som part thereof yit have I herd,/ In this matiere hou it hath ferd" (VI, 2437-40). At the beginning of Book Seven, he re-emphasizes his inability to be a good teacher about Aristotle because "it is noght to the matiere/ Of love, why we sitten hiere/ To schryve" (VII, 7-9).

    The juncture between Books Six and Seven seems to be unnecessary. Given the varying lengths of the books of the *Confessio*-- Book Five, for example, is 7844 lines long--Gower could have combined Books Six and Seven into a single book of 7878 lines, only 34 lines longer than Book Five. Had he done so, the lengthy digression that is Book Seven would simply have been a long narreme within Book Six, a fact which is emphasized because there is only one speech by Amans in Book Seven, twenty-two lines long, and the rest of the book is spoken by Genius. It is clear that Gower made Book Seven a separate unit in part to call attention to the relative unimportance of the Seven Deadly Sins compared to the theme of love itself. There are three main narremes in Book Seven: Genius' lengthy speech, ll. 1-5407, Amans' single speech, ll. 5408-29, and Genius' final speech, ll. 5430-38. The third functions both to conclude Book Seven and to introduce Book Eight, and the second--the only narreme in the book spoken by Amans--provides a contrast to the narremes spoken by Genius. Amans reintroduces the main theme of the *Confessio*, love: "Forthi, my goode fader diere,/ Lef al and speke of my matiere/ Touchende of love, as we begonne" (VII, 5421-23). By this device, Gower once more reminds us that Book Seven is a deliberate digression from the apparent thematic pattern of the *Confessio* even though it fits into the normal narremic pattern at the beginning and end. The explanation lies in the lower level of narrative structure, that indicated by the junctures between sections of Genius' speech.

    The junctures between sections of Genius' speech are indicated in Book Seven by Latin verses that comment on the material to follow, a form of juncture that often signals junctures not signalled by devices like a change of speaker. In Book Eight, for example, Gower introduces the first marginal incident--that dealing with the origin of mankind, the laws of marriage, and the stories of Caligula, Amon, and Lot and his daughters-- with a Latin quatrain, setting it off from the narreme about Appolinus by another quatrain. He then indicates the juncture between the first and second narremes by changing speakers from Genius to Amans and calling attention to the juncture by means of a Latin comment in the margin: "Confessio Amantis, vnde pro finali conclusione consilium Confessoris impetrat" (vol. II: 441) [The confession of Amans, as a result of which he obtains the advice of the Confessor for the last time]. This Latin comment calls attention to the importance of Amans' plea, "Youre hole conseil I beseche,/ That ye me be som weie teche/ What is my beste, as for an ende" (VIII, 2057-59), a plea which leads to the conclusion of the poem and

Amans' farewell to *amor*.

Gower introduces each marginal incident of Book Seven with Latin verses. The first, ll. 1-60, deals with "the Scole .../ Of Aristotle and ek the fare/ Of Alisandre" (VII, 3-5); Gower says that it will deal "chief of the Philosophie" (VII, 57). The second, ll. 61-202, deals with the "Theorique" (VII, 61) of Philosophy and the branches thereof, "Theologie" (VII, 73), "Phisique" (VII, 135), and "Mathematique" (VII, 146). The third, ll. 203-632, is the section that deals with the creation of the "foure elementz" (VII, 222) and their appearance among men as "complexions foure" (VII, 388), with the human "Soule diere" (VII, 492), and with "the thre parties" (VII, 532) of the earth. The fourth marginal incident, ll. 633-1506, deals with "the Planetes" (VII, 637), including astrological signs, "the sterres hihe" (VII, 1280), and "the science of Astronomie" (VII, 1439). The fifth, ll. 1507-1640, deals with the fact that "the hihe makere of natures/ The word to man hath yove above" (VII, 1508-9), and the sixth, ll. 1641-1710, deals with the "Practique" (VII, 1648) of Philosophy. The seventh, ll. 1711-1984, deals with the virtue of "trouthe" (VII, 1724) and includes the story known as King, Wine, Woman, and Truth and the tales of Apemen's daughter and Alceste. The eighth, ll. 1985-2694, deals with "largesse" (VII, 1989) and includes stories about Julius Caesar and "a worthi povere kniht" (VII, 2062), Antigonus and "Cinichus a povere kniht" (VII, 2119), Diogenes and "his felaw Arisippus" (VII, 2231), the Roman Triumph, the Emperor and "hise Macons" (VII, 2427), and "Achab .../ Which hadde al Irahel to rihte" (VII, 2529-30) and "a brothell, which Micheas hihte" (VII, 2595). The ninth, ll. 2695-3102, focuses on the importance of the "kinges governance" (VII, 2697) to promote justice in the realm and includes the stories of "Maximin" (VII, 2766), "Gayus Fabricius" (VII, 2784), the "Emperour Conrade" (VII, 2833), Carmidotoire, a "Romein/ Which Consul was of the Pretoire" (VII, 2846-47), "the grete king ... Cambises" (VII, 2893), "Ligurgius,/ Which of Athenis Prince was" (VII, 2918-19), and those "that ferst for rihtwisnesse/ Among the men the lawes made" (VII, 3044-45). The tenth, ll. 3103-4214, discusses "the vertu of Pite" (VII, 3107) and includes stories about "Constantin" (VII, 3137), "Codrus" (VII, 3183), and "Pompeie" (VII, 3215). It also discusses the converse, "crualte" (VII, 3249), exemplifying it with stories about "the tirant Leoncius" (VII, 3268), "Siculus" (VII, 3296), whom "no Pite myhte areste" (VII, 3298), "the grete tirant Dionys" (VII, 3341), "Lichaon" (VII, 3355), who "ayein the lawe of kinde/ Hise hostes slouh, and into mete/ He made her bodies" (VII, 3356-58), and "Duk ... Spertachus" (VII, 3418). Following the sections contrasting pity and cruelty, Genius points out that pity taken to an immoderate extreme is vicious, for pity must not "mesure excede" (VII, 3529). He exemplifies this point with the story of a mountain tormented by a mouse "in the londes of Archade" (VII, 3555) and with stories about "King Salomon" (VII, 3594), "Gedeon" (VII, 3633), "Saül" (VII, 3821) and "king Agag" (VII, 3823), David and his command that Solomon slay "Joab ... algate" (VII, 3863), "the king of Rome Lucius" (VII, 3946) and his fool, Solomon's successor, the foolish "Roboas" (VII, 4029), and "themperour Anthonius" (VII, 4181) and "Cipio, which hadde be/ Consul of Rome" (VII, 4187-88). The eleventh and last marginal incident, ll. 4215-5397, deals with "chastete" (VII, 4240) and includes positive and negative examples, "Sardana Pallus" (VII, 4314), "King David" (VII, 4345), "the king of Perse,/ That Cirus hihte" (VII, 4366-67), "Amalech the paien king" (VII, 4408), "Salomon, whos appetit/ Was holy set upon delit" (VII, 4477-78), "Anthonie" (VII, 4574), "the proude tirannyssh Romein/ Tarquinius" (VII, 4594-95) and his son "Arrons" (VII, 4598), who raped Lucrece, "Apius/ Whos other name is Claudius" (VII, 5131-32), who desired Virginia, and the marriage of "Sarra" (VII, 5315) and "Thobie" (VII, 5357).

    The content of the eleven marginal incidents of Book Seven is related in a close thematic way to the subject matter of the entire *Confessio*. The first six deal with philosophy and remind us that with a proper philosophical background, one can understand what lies behind worldly events: they prepare us for the conclusion of the poem. The sixth in particular--the structural center of the book--deals with "thre thinges" (VII, 1649) related to "the governance of kinges" (VII, 1650) and reminds us both that order and love are related in the microcosm of Amans and in the macrocosm of the realm and that the *Confessio* is "a bok for Engelondes sake" (Pro., 24). The last five marginal incidents of Book Seven call attention to what one might call the "Godly Virtues" of love, countering the fact that the *Confessio* seems to revolve around the Seven Deadly Sins against love, and the ninth--structurally the center of these five--deals with the "kinges governance" (VII, 2697). The other four sections deal with the courtly virtues of "trouthe" (VII, 1724), "largesse" (VII, 1989), "Pite" (VII, 3107), and "chastete" (VII, 4240) and help emphasize that the *Confessio* is about love and proper human relationships rather than sin.

    In Book Seven of the *Confessio*, Gower sets up a list of virtues that differs from the Seven Godly Virtues which in penitential works balance the Seven Deadly Sins. The *Confessio* therefore differs from Gower's *Mirour d'Omme* (see Olsson, "Cardinal Virtues"). Peck points out that in the *Mirour*, each of the Seven Deadly Sins has five daughters and that Gower "prescribes a remedy" (35) for each of the Sins; for example, the "remedy" for "Dame Orguil" is "Humilité" and that for her daughter "Ipocresie" is "Devocioun" (36). In the *Confessio*, Gower speaks of "the branches" (V, 7614) of the sins, and Genius promises "the branches [of Avarice] schifte/ Be ordre" (V, 4668-69). As Peck observes, Gower uses a classification system like that in the *Mirour* only in Books One, Two, and Three (see 37), to which I would like to add the fact that Gower warns us in Book Six that he intends to treat only "tuo" (VI, 13) of the branches. Peck says that even when Gower uses the *Mirour*'s system "meticulously" in the *Confessio* "he does so with flexibility" (37). The effect of the scheme in the *Mirour* is to emphasize virtue and sin; the effect of the presentation in the *Confessio* is to emphasize love.

An awareness of the marginal incidents of Book Seven shows that Gower is concerned with the relationship between the courtly and the theological virtues. Although Gower is writing for an English court speaking both English and Anglo-Norman and behaving in accordance with a code of manners developed on the continent, a code which was originally intended to identify and maintain the privileges of a small aristocratic class, he does not use courtly virtues to help maintain those aristocratic privileges. Like his use of the language and manners of courtly love, his use of the courtly virtues is intended to reinforce the theological virtues and promote man's relationship with God. Nevertheless, an understanding of the courtly virtues is essential for a proper interpretation of Book Seven and of the *Confessio* as a whole, and Gower must have deliberately chosen to use the seventh book of his poem to describe the remedies for the Seven Deadly Sins against love.

The fact that "largesse" is one of the virtues discussed and that the stories involve imperial characters and the philosopher Arisippe who "his bok aside/ Hath leid, and to the court he wente" (VII, 2248-49) indicates that Gower intends to explore courtly virtues. According to the thirteenth-century didactic poet Robert de Blois, "largesce" (125: 1145) is "Roïne/ Sor totes les autres vertuz" (125: 1148-49) [Queen over all the other virtues] and "totes vertuz enlumine" (125: 1147) [illuminates all virtues]. Furthermore, "largesce" promotes virtue and provides remedies for vice analogous to those provided by the Seven Godly Virtues in works like the *Mirour*:

> [Largesce] li malvais vice tuit,
> Orgoil, descorde et felonie
> Et covoitise et male envie
> S'en fuent, ne puent durer
> Ou largesce suet converser.
> Car largesce si grant leu tient,
> Que de li naist et de li vient
> Concorde, pais, humilitez,
> Amors et debonairetez.
> (125-26: 1154-62)

> [Largesse slays evil vice; pride, discord, treachery, avarice, and evil envy flee away and do not dare to stay where largesse is found, because from her is born and from her

come concord, peace, humility, love, and nobility.]

Peck notes that liberality is "the *Mirour*'s antidote to Avarice" (144), and in the *Confessio*, Avarice "stant in contraire to Largesse" (V, 7656). Genius recommends that Amans be "large of ... despence" (V, 4869)--although not prodigal (see V, 7770-71)--as a cure for Avarice, commenting later that Avarice "Largesse/ ... mai non ... abregge" (VII, 1989-90). The courtly connotations of "largesse" in the *Confessio* make it a remedy for a much broader range of sins than Avarice alone--including pride--as well as the source of courtly and Christian virtues.

It is clear from writers like Robert de Blois that "largesse," although the "Queen" of courtly virtues, does not exist in isolation but is part of a complex of virtues. The same is true of Gower, who in fact places "largesse" after the virtue of "trouthe" (VII, 1724), defining the latter as "the vertu soverein of alle" (VII, 1776). As a courtly virtue, "trouthe" is a complex term; John Stevens points out that in Chaucer's *Franklin's Tale*, it has several meanings: "a pledged word, the promise that you give another person; ... integrity, the truth to your own inmost self; ... [and] loyalty, the bond of dependence that keeps society stable and united ...; [and it is] a philosophical and religious term for the ultimate reality, ... the universal principle by which the Universe is governed" (64-65). In the heroic society of the early Middle Ages, "trouthe" meant that a person must keep his promises literally or be, to quote a *hapax legomenon* from *Beowulf*, a "treowloga" (Klaeber, 107: 2847a) [troth-lier; one false to his pledged word]. Since oaths were what held both the heroic and the feudal societies together (see, for example, Ganshof, 27-30 and 70-72), such "trouthe" was an important courtly concept, one Gower explores in the tale of Florent in Book One. At its worst, "trouthe" can imply contractual obligation in a legalistic sense that can be at odds with both courtly and Christian behavior. At its best, however, "trouthe" is guided, not only by the idea that words and deeds should coincide, but also by adherence to the higher spiritual authority of the Church. In the *Confessio*, "trouthe" is the "vertu soverein" (VII, 1776) because it provides the remedy for all the sins against love and against social order.

The Romance of the Rose shows that pity is one of the complex of courtly virtues.[4] As Fragment B of the Middle English translation says, the despondent lover is helped when "were come of grace, by God sent,/ Fraunchise, and with hir Pite" (Chaucer, 598: 3500-1), and pity is one of the virtues that helps him kiss the Rosebud. In the *Mirour*, "pites" is merely the remedy for "homicide," one of the branches of "ire" (see Peck, 36); in the *Confessio*, "pite" (VII, 3107) is clearly a virtue appropriate for both the earthly court of Constantine and the heavenly court of Christ, whose Incarnation, as Peck observes, shows us that He "took ... pity upon mankind" (149). Stevens notes that the word "pitee" is "associated with religious feeling through Latin *pietas* and Old French *pitié, piété*, on the one hand, and with courtly manners (it is coupled with 'debonairtee', 'gentilesse' and 'womanly benignitee') on the other" (71) [italics Stevens']. In both forms, it represents a "civilizing" influence that is not "confined to individuals as individuals ... [but] is directed towards producing more agreeable people for society" (Stevens, 50) and people of greater moral virtue. In both its senses, it is a useful term in the *Confessio*, which merges courtly and Christian ideals and language rather than, like the *Mirour*, viewing virtue in a narrow sense. Book Seven of the *Confessio* helps place Gower in a tradition of romance writing that goes back to twelfth-century writers like Chrétien de Troyes.

Gower's choice of the fourth courtly virtue, "chastete" (VII, 4240), also places him in the tradition of Chrétien. Peck notes that Gower uses Chastity as a word with a broader meaning than we normally apply to it in the twentieth century. In the *Mirour d'Omme*, Gower identifies Chastity as "the antidote for Luxure" (Peck, 150), but the courtly context in which the virtue appears in Book Seven of the *Confessio*--following three other courtly virtues and exemplified by the behavior of royal personages--shows that it has a broader definition than that noted by Peck. Although scholars influenced by Lewis' *The Allegory of Love* view courtly love as basically adulterous and therefore unchaste, recent research has shown that such was not the case. William Calin points out that many medieval works depict a love ending in marriage and that many scholars do not believe that medieval literature idealizes adultery. He argues that terms like "*fin'amor* or *bon amor* ... designate secular, profane, heterosexual love" (33) [italics Calin's] that involves "highly intense, passionate, personal involvement between two people of opposite sexes" (35) rather than adultery. As a result, chastity is a courtly virtue equally appropriate to Chrétien's *Cligés* or *Erec et Enide* and to the *Confessio*.

Structurally, the *Confessio Amantis* is a work carefully ordered to promote love--both *amor* and *caritas*--and virtue--both courtly and Christian. Although both *caritas* and Christian virtue are more important than *amor* and courtly virtue, the latter are necessary because they lead a person to the former. On a structural level, the *Confessio* resembles Chrétien's romances, in which "a knight, successful in the eyes of the world, suffers a moral or spiritual humiliation" (Topsfield, 25). He then seeks "rehabilitation" and finally "progresses beyond the values and reputation of his former self, and attains a degree of virtue and wholeness beyond that of the ideal Arthurian knight, such as Gawain" (Topsfield, 25). Amans makes an analogous progression, although he passes beyond the best of secular values. Far from being a digressive collection of tales only loosely ordered by a framework of the Seven Deadly Sins, the *Confessio* is a structurally tight work whose message is the same as that given by Kynde to Will the Dreamer in *Piers Plowman*: "Lerne to love, ... and leef alle othere" (Langland, 257: XX: 208). The tightness of the structure of the *Confessio* extends down to the linguistic details of the way that the tales are told.

Chapter Three

Puns and the Language of Poetry
in the *Confessio Amantis*

Gower's fame in the twentieth century rests on what Macaulay has called his "unquestionable talent for story-telling" (Gower, vol. I: xii) rather than on his poetic talent. Although Douglas Gray has noted Gower's literary artistry and has observed that "his lines have a genuine polish, and a sense of verbal melody" (316), and Fernand Mossé says that Gower "manages his octosyllabics with sure mastery" (314), many readers would agree with Macaulay that Gower's poetry is "shallow" (Gower, vol. I: xii). Even though Macaulay finds instances of "style and poetical qualities" (Gower, vol. I: xiii) to praise in the *Confessio*, the spareness and succinctness of the narratives lead many to conclude that Gower's writing is basically "prosaic" (Lewis, 201). Lewis points out, however, that Gower's revisions in the *Confessio* demonstrate "the working of a fine, and finely self-critical, poetic impulse" (204), adducing as evidence Gower's revision of the description of the "ladis" (IV, 1307) in the tale of Rosiphelee (see 204).
    Minnis notes that "the composite and compendious nature of [the] *Confessio Amantis* is antithetical to post-Romantic notions of poetic unity" ("Introduction" 1). The judgments on Gower as a poet resemble those passed on other medieval poets, who have been criticized by those who are predisposed to believe that poetry must be metaphoric (see Brewer, "Some Metonymic Relationships" 37). On this assumption, Gower's poetry, which is basically non-metaphoric, is prosaic--indeed, is almost prose. In a study of linguistic structures, Roman Jakobson points out that "the development of a discourse may take place along two different semantic lines: one topic may lead to another either through their similarity or through their contiguity. The metaphoric way would be the most appropriate term for the first case and the metonymic way for the second, since they find their most condensed expression in metaphor and metonymy respectively" (123).
    Following the Romantic and Symbolist critics of poetry, Jakobson states that "the principle of similarity underlies poetry. ... Prose, on the contrary, is forwarded essentially by contiguity. Thus, for poetry, metaphor, and for prose, metonymy is the line of least resistance and, consequently, the study of poetical tropes is directed chiefly toward metaphor" (127). Derek Brewer, however, pointing out that Chaucer's poetry is not exclusively metaphoric although it is highly poetical, argues that Jakobson's identification of the metonymic principle of linguistic construction can help us understand the "associative" or "metonymic structures ... within Chaucer's poetry" ("Some Metonymic Relationships" 41). Brewer, not only suggests that metonymy is an identifiable part of some poetic structures,

but also argues that an understanding of it in the work of Chaucer can help us understand the poetical nature of works by other medieval authors. An understanding of metonymy helps us understand the poetical nature of the *Confessio*, as critics overly influenced by Romantic and Symbolist readings have been unable to do. Discussing Chaucer, Brewer suggests that "various ways of exploring metonymic structures suggest themselves, both at a close verbal level, and on a broader scale" ("Some Metonymic Relationships" 41); I wish first to discuss examples from the "close verbal level" of the *Confessio*.

An important aspect of Gower's poetical art involves his use of puns to call attention to contiguous ideas. Because his use is pervasive, one must conclude that he uses puns deliberately to underscore themes and evoke ideas. As Paull F. Baum says, puns are non-metaphoric because "the two meanings remain distinct" whereas "in metaphor the two elements are fused" ("Chaucer's Puns" 227). Punning--"association by sound affinity" (Koestler, 314) [italics deleted]--is related to the use of rhyme, alliteration, and assonance (see Koestler, 314-16) and to poetic creativity in general. To understand that Gower's puns can be analyzed semiotically and categorized in terms of both their structure and their literary nature, one must apply the studies of modern linguists to literary punning.

Puns are by nature ambiguous, and L. G. Kelly points out that many people consider ambiguity "an undesirable, if not pathological, state in language" (5). James Brown has identified eight types of literary puns, and Archibald A. Hill has studied "the reality of literary punning" (373); puns have been studied in *Beowulf* (see Anne Harris), in the Harley lyrics (see Harrington, Ransom, and Reiss), and in the works of Langland (see Huppé, Ryan, "Word Play" and *Langland*, and Tristram), Chaucer (see Baum, "Chaucer's Puns" and "Chaucer's Puns: A Supplementary List," Kökeritz, and Rowland), and Shakespeare (see Muir, "Shakespeare" and "Uncomic Pun").[1] Such studies demonstrate that puns are an important part of a poet's literary artistry; in the case of *Piers Plowman*, for example, Maureen Quilligan has shown that puns are related to the allegory and that Langland's exploration of the polysemantic nature of language aids the didactic purpose of the poem.

Like Langland, Gower uses puns consciously as part of his poetic technique. His use of puns has been overlooked by most scholars just as his literary artistry in general has been, and the modern translation by Terence Tiller omits puns to make the *Confessio* conform to modern ideas about poetics (see Ito, *John Gower* 247). Masayoshi Ito speaks with respect about Gower's puns, and Peck observes that Gower draws a moral from the tale of Virginia in Book Seven that "is built on a pun: 'And thus thunchaste was chastised'" (157) and suggests that the pun helps Gower emphasize that unchastity (typified in Book Eight by incest) represents sinfulness. Winthrop Wetherbee argues that Gower uses a pun on "braieth" in the tale of Nebuchadnezzar's Dream to underscore the repentance of Nebuchadnezzar (see 256). These puns typify Gower's use of the technique, and a close study shows Gower's artistry.

Before discussing the poetic effect of puns in the *Confessio*, one must first grant that they are indeed found therein, because "it is not only the speaker who can make a pun, but the receiver or interpreter as well" (Sherzer, 345). I should like to mention an illustrative example which, like the puns identified by Peck and Wetherbee, is metonymically appropriate to its context in the *Confessio*. In Book Eight, Venus tells Amans to act in a manner appropriate to his age because "olde grisel is no fole" (VIII, 2407), and since "grisel" means "a grey horse," the line says that an old grey horse is not a foal and the elderly Amans should cease acting like a young man. The Middle English word "fole" also means, however, "fool," a meaning appropriate to the line because wisdom, not folly, should characterize an old man, and a sensible old man does not play the fool by acting like a foal.

Brown argues that "the pun effect is a semantic achievement and derives from the symbolic nature of language" (14) and that "one necessary condition for pun perception ... is previous knowledge of multiple and disparate meanings for the pun word" (14-15). A modern scholar must read the *Confessio* with care to determine whether and where "multiple and disparate meanings" of Middle English words apply. In Book Seven, for example, Genius speaks of Lichaon, who "ayein the lawe of kinde/ Hise hostes slouh, and into mete/ He made her bodies to ben ete" (VII, 3356-58). To punish him, Jupiter "fro mannes forme/ Into a wolf him let transforme:/ And thus the crualte was kidd" (VII, 3363-65). Although "kidd" is the past participle of "kythen" and means "made known," it also suggests the word "kidde" [the young of a goat]. If the pun were indeed present, it would be contextually appropriate to the tale of Lichaon: Lichaon is transformed into a wolf to match his nature because he has treated his fellow human beings like domestic animals to be devoured.

In another case from Book Seven, Gower names the four horses of the chariot of the Sun; according to Fulgentius, the third is Lampos (see Macaulay, vol. II: 524). Gower substitutes the name "Lampes" (VII, 856), leading a modern reader to wonder whether his choice was influenced by the plural of the common noun "lamp(e)." Such a choice would have been appropriate for one of the horses of the Sun "that bringen lyht unto this erthe" (VII, 858); Gower describes the first, Eritheüs, as a horse "which is red and schyneth hote" (VII, 854) and the second as "Acteos the bryhte" (VII, 855). Medieval authors often pun on names; Anne Leslie Harris studies the *Beowulf* poet's use thereof to "call attention to his themes" (414), and Roger Dragonetti suggests that Chrétien de Troyes puns consciously on the names of Arthurian characters. Dragonetti admits that his reading "reste finalement problématique" (188), and a modern critic must always proceed with caution. Nevertheless, there are places in the *Confessio* where perception of such puns deepens the reader's appreciation of the poem.

One difficulty that the critic interested in the literary effect of puns encounters is that "the metalinguistic vocabulary for forms of speech play ... is not as precise as careful analysis would require" (Sherzer, 347). A pun is "the bisociation of a single phonetic form with two meanings--two strings of thought tied together by an acoustic knot" (Koestler, 64-65) or, more generally, it is a "form of speech play in which a word or phrase unexpectedly and simultaneously combines two unrelated meanings" (Sherzer, 336). Ricardian England was a period when puns were used "for serious effects" (Ong, 315), unlike the twentieth century when, as Joel Sherzer observes, they are often considered "humorous in intention" and "inappropriate for serious discourse" (345). It is not, therefore, surprising to find puns in the *Confessio*.

One sign that Gower intends the puns to be a part of the "lore" of the poem is the presence of puns in the Prologue. Because Gower alerts us to the fact that "this prologue is so assised/ That it to wisdom al belongeth" (Pro., 66-67) in contrast to the remainder of the *Confessio*, the puns are intended in part to "belong" to "wisdom." I should like to note that Gower's "To King Henry the Fourth: In Praise of Peace" (see Gower, vol. II: 481-94), whose purpose is serious, includes no puns, although it uses a few of the punning rhymes ("rimes équivoques") to be discussed in chapter four, such as the verb "reule" (488: 258) [rule a kingdom] and the noun "reule" (488: 259) [regulation or custom]. The presence of puns in the *Confessio* suggests that they are the kind of embellishment that also contributes to the "lust" of the poem.

In the Prologue, Gower says that love "many a *wys* man hath put under./ And in this *wyse* I thenke trete/ Towardes hem that now be grete" (Pro., 76-78) [italics mine], and the presence of "wys" in l. 76 makes it possible to read "wyse" in l. 77 as a pun meaning "wise manner" rather than just "manner." He repeats the pun for emphasis in the first encapsulated narrative of the *Confessio*, the tale of Nebuchadnezzar's Dream, stating that God "hath his prophecie sent,/ In such a wise" (Pro., 588-89) as he will recount. Because he later calls Daniel "the wiseste of Caldee" (Pro., 666), the pun suggests that Gower intends to recount the story in a "wise manner." It is especially reasonable to interpret "wyse/wise" as a pun because Gower uses "rimes équivoques" of "wise" [manner] and "wise" [wise] in various places (see VIII, 371-72 and 1649-50, for example) (see discussion in chapter four).

In the Prologue, Gower uses a number of other puns that contribute to the "lore" of the Prologue and of the *Confessio* as a whole. One of the most allusive raises the Boethian question of the nature of true and false goods and contrasts "the feith of Crist and alle goode/ Thurgh hem that thanne were goode/ And sobre and chaste and large and wyse" (Pro., 237-38) to the "worldes good, which may noght laste" (Pro., 249). By using puns, Gower calls attention to ideas and themes that he intends to explore in both the frame story of the *Confessio* and the encapsulated tales, making the didactic level of the *Confessio* clear before turning to the "lust" of the tales.

In order to discuss puns, one must be aware of the use thereof in ordinary speech. Harvey Sacks observes that "it is plain that at least one sense of how puns work involves the presence of a word, phrase, or other construction of more than one meaning, one meaning being used in understanding the construction in its conversational locus; while the other meaning(s) are also fitted to the locus, although in different ways" (139). Furthermore, L. G. Heller argues that "what has largely gone unrecognized ... is the fact that the 'pun' represents not just one pattern but rather an entire class of different patterns which all share the following structural characteristic: ... a single manifesting mark signals more than one conceptual function" (271). I should like to suggest that a pun is dependent upon contiguity for its effect because it is based on what Brewer calls "'chain', 'association', [or] sequence'" rather than on the "'choice'" or "'likeness' (including contrast)" ("Some Metonymic Relationships" 40) characteristic of metaphor.[2]

Brown argues that "the meaning of a word is, fundamentally, its context" (17) and that a pun works by "the linking of contexts" (16) that would normally be disparate, that is, by an effect I call metonymic because it is contiguous. He further argues that "context-linking" is significant because of its "influence upon total context; the pun asserts a complex, non-lexical meaning which functions to define total meaning. The context-linking ... is an organic combination or amalgam of what we ordinarily consider to be disparate (even contradictory) meanings for a word" (17). He points out that most puns "link only two contexts" and "make use of only two meanings for the pun word" (18). The example quoted above, "olde grisel is no fole" (VIII, 2407), typifies such a "simple pun," in which "the multiple meanings ... appear within one syntactical situation" (Brown, 19) and "the variable pun meaning is literal to both the syntax and sense of the sentence" (Brown, 19). Both "foal" and "fool" fit the sentence syntactically and make equally good sense in it. However, when one considers the larger context of Venus' speech--using context in the general sense of the word rather than in the specialized sense meant by Brown--the meaning "foal" is the literal meaning intended, but "fool" is appropriate to the sentence for metonymic reasons.

According to Brown, another type of pun occurs when "the variable pun meaning is metaphoric to both the syntax and sense of the sentence"

(20). This type is found in the line "And thus the crualte was kidd" (VII, 3365), assuming that the pun discussed above is indeed to be found therein. In this line, the meaning "known" is that which fits both the syntax and the sense of the sentence; the context of the story, however, makes it possible for a reader to perceive an allusion to a "kid," which deepens our understanding of the tale of Lichaon. Brown argues that a pun is "a symbolic device which can force us from the pragmatic realm of direct experience into the complex realm of abstractions, the magnificent realm of fantasy" (15). A modern reader realizes that part of the effect of the puns in the Prologue is to introduce the fantasy world of the *Confessio* and to prepare us for a "realm of abstractions" in which it seems as if anything can happen. The puns which are frequently used in the *Confessio* also contribute to the fantastic in the poem.

Brown suggests that when members of an audience "read (or listen) carefully, failure to perceive a pun is impossible" (15). This fact raises problems for the modern reader of the *Confessio* because it is difficult to be certain which puns would have been perceived by medieval readers and when, especially bearing in mind Claes Schaar's warning that medieval readers "did not look for ... [puns] to the same extent as we do" and that "those they looked for were of a different kind" (161-62). A modern reader can be confident that a pun exists in the *Confessio* when the same pun is found in other Middle English works. Edmund Reiss has perceived a pun operative in the lyric "Foweles in the frith," whose narrator expresses the "mulch sorw" he feels "for beste of bon and blod." Reiss suggests that the pun shows that the lyric is "religious ... in its expression of human isolation" (19). He argues that "to be a beast ... of bone and blood means ... to experience *mulch sorw*" (19-20) [italics Reiss's] and "to be the 'best' of bone and blood" means "to be man, ... [separated] from the rest of nature" (20).

Our perception of this pun raises some difficulties because the words were not homophones but were "differentiated by the length of the vowel" (Moser, 336). Nevertheless, linguists have shown that puns that are not fully homophonous are indeed puns. Walter Nash observes that such puns are "phonetic similitudes" which "bend the rules of punning" (139.) Heller points out that one important criterion for puns "from the point of view of audience reaction is that of absolute versus only partial identity of the manifesting units correlated with the functions. ... In appropriate contexts, even a partial rather than complete identity of manifesting units suffices to suggest correlations with functions normally associated with slightly different manifestations" (275). A famous example of this kind of pun is Hamlet's desire that "this too too solid/sullied flesh would melt" (see Shakespeare, 44: 129). Thomas C. Moser, Jr., suggests that the author of "Foweles in the frith" "almost certainly had a pun in mind" although it is difficult to determine "which sense was primary and which was secondary"

(336) and to make literary judgments about the poem.

In contrast to Reiss, I interpret "Foweles in the frith" as a secular love lyric whose narrator plays on the fact that the lady deserves the superlative "best" but has a physical nature that he can hope to possess.[3] This interpretation receives confirmation from the fact that Gower uses the same pun in a sophisticated manner, calling attention to it in the tale of Mundus and Paulina. Paulina is "the beste" (I, 768) of the women in Rome, but when she learns that she has spent the night with Duke Mundus rather than with "the god Anubus" (I, 836), she laments, "I am non other than a beste,/ Now I defouled am of tuo" (I, 976-77). The treachery of Mundus and the priests of Isis makes Paulina feel like a beast instead of like the best of women, although her husband comforts her and their friends believe it is "for the beste" (I, 997) to complain to the emperor. In "Foweles in the frith," the use of "beste" represents what Brown identifies as the "most common" (19) type of simple pun, one in which both meanings--in this case, the common noun "beast" and the substantivized adjective "best"--fit both the syntax and the sense of the sentence. In the tale of Mundus and Paulina, in contrast, each sentence permits only one meaning of the word to fit the sense and syntax at any particular time. The pun operates within the metonymic web of allusions established by the tale as a whole and is "a symbolic device" (Brown, 15) that calls attention to an idea important in the tale.

In some contexts in which "beste" is used in the *Confessio*, the word has only a single meaning. When Nestor warns Demephon and Athemas that they will be kings "wher no lif is bot only beste" (III, 1821) and that it is wrong "to se the wilde beste wone/ Wher whilom duelte a mannes Sone" (III, 1829-30), "beste" means unambiguously "beast"; in a prayer in a discussion of the Crusades ("Godd do thereof amendement/ So as he wot what is the beste" [III, 2514-15]), it means unambiguously "best." In other contexts, the pun is operative and underlines ideas expressed. Gower's most striking use of the pun occurs in the tale of Florent, and it derives some of its impact from the presence of the same pun in the tale of Mundus and Paulina, which precedes the tale of Florent. After offering to tell him the answer that will save his life if he promises to marry her, the Loathly Lady tells Florent to offer first the answer he has collected that he thinks is the "beste" (I, 1603). Because it turns out to be the worst of answers--that is, an answer that will not save his life--Florent uses the answer given him by the Loathly Lady, the answer that is truly the best. After returning home, he tells his "prive conseil" (I, 1738) that he "nedes moste/ This beste wedde to his wif" (I, 1740-41). As the description of the "olde wyht" (I, 1672) makes clear, she is more than "the lothlieste what/ That evere man caste on his yhe" (I, 1676-77). Even when "arraied to the beste" (I, 1748) [dressed in the best manner or as the beast], she is truly bestial in appearance with "hire

Nase bass, hire browes hyhe,/ Hire yhen smal and depe set" (I, 1678-79) and "hire Necke ... schort" (I, 1687). After Florent surrenders his sovereignty to her, however, she becomes "the faireste of visage/ That evere in al this world he syh" (I, 1804-5), deserving of the superlative adjective "beste." The Loathly Lady changes from a beast to the "best" of women because of magic and the loyalty of Florent to his word, and she gives him advice that is "best" for both of them when he does not know "the beste" (I, 1817) course of action to choose. It is only in retrospect that the audience perceives the pun in l. 1741 and realizes that it is a simple pun like that in "Foweles in the frith" which fits both the sense and the syntax of the sentence.

Knowledge of multiple meanings of a word in other Middle English works can cause problems for a reader who is looking for puns and paying insufficient attention to the context within which a word is found in the *Confessio*. In Middle English, "fode" is used in the sense of a nurseling or other child and, more generally, of any person (see the reference to Athulf in *King Horn*, French-Hale, vol. I: 64: 1340). The Wakefield Master makes effective use of the two meanings of "fode" in the *Secunda Pastorum* when the Secundus Pastor addresses the infant Christ as "frely foyde" (Cawley, 62: 720), the noble child who is being nursed by his mother who will become the Eucharist, the noble food of Christians. When Gower speaks of Gluttony, however, he uses "fode" to mean simply "food," as when Amans says, "So comth hope in ate laste,/ Whan I non other fode knowe" (VI, 888-89). Reading "fode" as a pun suggesting the beloved lady would violate the sense of the passage and the integrity of the *Confessio*. The critic interested in studying puns in the *Confessio* must, therefore, be careful to guide his interpretation by the context in which the words are used, especially since Gower often calls attention to puns by repetition, as he does by using the pun on "beste" in the tales both of Mundus and Paulina and of Florent. There are three contexts in which puns are found in the *Confessio*: sometimes they reinforce the theme or themes of a particular tale or part of the frame story, sometimes those of the book in which the passage appears, and sometimes those of the *Confessio* as a whole.

The first encapsulated tale in Book One is that of Acteon, a tale "Ovide telleth in his bok" (I, 333) that provides "ensample touchende of mislok" (I, 334). As Peter G. Beidler shows, Gower changes Ovid's story so that Acteon is an active hunter who is deliberately guilty of "mislok," contributing "to a sense of poetic justice when the prideful hunter becomes the desperate hunted by the end of the story" (Beidler, "Tale of Acteon" 9). In addition, Gower uses an important pun to emphasize that the hunter becomes the hunted, that of "hert" [hart] and "hert" [heart]. This pun is found in numerous Middle English works, including *The Book of the Duchess*, in which the "hert-huntyng" (Chaucer, 279: 1313) alludes both to the hunt of the "hert" (Chaucer, 270: 351) and to the Man in Black's courtship of "goode faire White" (Chaucer, 276: 948) (see Baum, "Chaucer's Puns" 239, Carson, and Grennen, "*Hert-huntyng*"); it may indeed be a "triple pun" (Prior, 3) on hart, heart, and hurt. In the *Confessio*, Diana "forschop [Acteon] anon, and the liknesse/ Sche made him taken of an Hert" (I, 370-71), and "this Hert his oghne houndes slowhe" (I, 377). Shortly thereafter, Genius warns Amans, "Be war of thin heringe,/ Which to the *Herte* the tidinge/ Of many a vanite hath broght" (I, 449-51) [italics mine]. I should like to suggest that an audience would remember the earlier use of the word "hert" and would be attuned to the pun thereon used by other poets of the late medieval period and that Gower chose to make the tale of Acteon the first encapsulated tale of the *Confessio* proper specifically because so doing enabled him to use the pun on "hert." The pun is appropriate both to the tale and to the theme of the misuse of love in the *Confessio* as a whole and works by alluding to larger themes of the tale and the poem rather than as a simple pun, for in each case, only one meaning is appropriate to the syntax and sense of the given sentence.

Throughout the *Confessio*, Gower uses puns that are appropriate to their contexts in their respective tales and in the *Confessio*. Some of the most noteworthy occur in the last tale, that of Appolinus. One important theme of the tale is the Sea Voyage that is life, a theme Gower emphasizes by his use of the type-scene of the Sea Voyage that he inherited from the English poetic tradition (see chapter five). When shipwrecked on the shores of Pentapolim, naked and alone, Appolinus "wiste of himself no *bote*" (VIII, 639) [italics mine]. The literal meaning of the line is that Appolinus knew no *remedy* for himself, but since "bote" is also the oblique form of "bot," the line suggests a pun appropriate for the context: Appolinus knows of no remedy for his troubles because he has lost his "bot" and all the goods and men therein that would have assured him a royal welcome. Because the meaning "boat" does not fit the sentence syntactically, this pun is not like that on "fole" in Book Eight or that on "beste" in "Foweles in the frith" and the tale of Florent. Instead, it is the kind of pun that Brown points out occurs when "the variable meaning of the pun word is metaphoric to the syntax and literal to the sense of the sentence" (20) and when the "conditions call for the literal acceptance of two meanings which are incompatible" (20).

Because the theme of the Sea Voyage of life is important, not only in the tale of Appolinus, but also in the *Confessio* as a whole, Gower uses puns that allude thereto in places other than Book Eight. The simplest occurs in Genius' discussion of the sacrilege committed by lovers, in which he says that "so nyh the weder thei wol love" (V, 7048). As Macaulay notes, "this is a nautical metaphor, 'so near the wind will they steer'" and "the verb 'love' is the modern 'luff'" (Gower, vol. II: 509), and "luff" is clearly the meaning most appropriate to both syntax and sense. Although Macaulay asserts that "the rhyme with 'glove' makes 'love' from 'lufian' out of the question, even if it gave a satisfactory sense" (Gower, vol. II: 509), I would argue that he is not taking into account Gower's use of puns. The verb "love" is appropriate to the sentence syntactically just as the verb "luff" is because each is the stem of a verb which can follow the modal verb "wol." In addition, it is metonymically appropriate to the sentence, because those who love "nyh the weder" are those who seek to "finde here love" (V, 7039) in a place inappropriate for conducting a love affair, a "holi place" (V, 7042). The use of the noun "love" in l. 7039 makes a reader predisposed to interpret the verb "love" in l. 7048 as a pun meaning both "luff" and "love." This reading provides an example of the kind of pun defined by Brown as that in which "the variable meaning of the pun word is literal to the syntax and metaphoric to the sense of the sentence" (20), which he says "might be called the allegorical pun" (20).

In a passage in the tale of Philemenis involving a literal Sea Voyage which alludes to the theme of the Sea Voyage of life, Gower describes the funeral of "Pantasilee of Amazoine" (IV, 2166) with a pun. A reader's appreciation of it depends on his or her sensitivity to morphemes and the way in which compounds are made in English. After "Pirrus the Sone of Achilles" (IV, 2161) has slain Pantasilee, Philemenis takes her body and the surviving Amazons "forth in his *Schip*" (IV, 2170) [italics mine]:

> Thei aryve;
> Wher that the body was begrave
> With *worschipe*, and the wommen save.
> And for the *goodschipe* of this dede
> Thei granten hem a lusti mede.
> (IV, 2170-74) [italics mine]

In both "worschipe" and "goodschipe," "-schipe" is a derivational morpheme meaning the quality or condition of the first element of the word. By punning on the literal "Schip," which alludes to the Sea Voyage of life, and on the derivational morpheme, Gower suggests the importance in life of the moral virtues of goodness and honorable behavior. As in the case of the pun on "wyse/wise" in the Prologue, that on "-schipe" and "Schipe" is reinforced by Gower's use of the words as the rhyming elements in numerous couplets (see discussion in chapter four).

Gower often uses etymological puns, apparently on the assumption that they will be of interest to his audience. Etymological puns present a special problem for the modern reader because they "are etymologically 'opaque' to anyone who has no smattering of Latin or Greek" (Nash, 144). Furthermore, modern readers are not predisposed to enjoy such puns because they regard them as "pretentious" and "pedantic" (Nash, 144). Since Gower is writing for an audience whose most educated members would be familiar with both Latin and Anglo-Norman, he uses puns that depend on a knowledge of languages other than English for their effect. Near the beginning of Book One, for example, Amans says that he seeks "the rihte salve of such a Sor" (I, 33), and the meaning of "salve" appropriate to both the sense and the syntax of the line is that of the English word which means "a healing ointment." One acquainted with Latin, however, will think of the imperative singular of the verb "salveo." The meaning of "salve," "give a salutation of greeting," is appropriate to the sense of the line and metonymically appropriate to the syntax because it reminds us that the "salve" for a lover's "Sor" is the greeting of his lady. Although the form of "salve" that Gower uses is "salue" (see II, 1504, for example), I would argue that a Middle English audience would be aware of the English/Latin pun, especially since authors use puns that involve an appreciation of the close phonemic relationship between "u" and "v" in English. For example, in *Piers Plowman* B, XIV: 219, Langland uses the line "Ne have *powere* in *pouerte* if pacyence it folwe" (see Ryan, *Langland*, 136) [italics Ryan's]. Gower uses the same pun in the tale of Alexander and the Pirate; the pirate, who leads "a *povere* route" (III, 2386) [italics mine], says, "If the *pouer* were myn,/ Mi will is most in special/ To rifle" (III, 2382-84) [italics mine]. He also warns that a rich and powerful man "tomorwe ... mai be *povere*" (III, 2399) [italics mine] whereas a "*povere* man" (III, 2401) [italics mine] may achieve "gret richesse" (III, 2401). The semi-homophonic pun on "pouer" and "povere" reminds a reader of the theme of Fortune's Wheel in the *Confessio*.

When Gower uses puns in a tale, he usually calls attention to the rhetorical importance of punning by using more than one. The axial pun in the tales of Mundus and Paulina and of Florent is that on "beste" [best] and "beste" [beast], but both tales involve other puns. Mundus' name is an etymological pun on Latin "mundus" [world] and English "mund" [hand or protection]. Gower suggests that Mundus' evil rule is related to his worldly use of his hands to seduce rather than protect one of his citizens. Mundus "wolde his *thonk* pourchace" (I, 816) [italics mine], a simple pun appropriate to both sense and syntax: "thonk" means both "will" and "reward," the reward of a lover's service being the favors of the lady. Gower adds a level to the pun because Mundus literally purchases the favors of Paulina by bribing the priests--"to ech of hem yaf thanne a yifte" (I, 817)--and rewarding them for doing his will. Paulina "was afterward engined" (I, 878), another simple pun, because "engined" means both "deceived" and "entrapped." When the crime is known, there is "juise" (I, 1047) for both Mundus and the priests. Since "juise" means both "judgment" and "punishment," and since the judgment is that the men be punished, both meanings fit the sense and the syntax.

As in the tale of Mundus and Paulina, the puns in the tale of Florent form clusters that call attention to important themes. When Florent first encounters the Loathly Lady, "sche *cleped* him" (I, 1535) [italics mine]-- called him and "clipped" or seized him--and after marriage, she "*clepeth* him hire housebonde" (I, 1768) [italics mine]--"calls" him her husband and embraces him as her husband. Later, "in armes sche beclipte hire lord" (I, 1790)--embraced the man she called lord. She says, "My lord, go we to bedde,/ For I to that entente *wedde*" (I, 1769-70) [italics mine]. Since "wedde" is a verb meaning both "to pledge or promise" and, specifically, "to contract a marriage covenant," and since the Loathly Lady has made a covenant with Florent that involves their subsequent marriage, both meanings of the verb are operative in the sentence.

The puns on "clepen" and "wedde" are simple puns, but some of the puns in the tale of Florent are of a different kind, being metonymically appropriate to the sense of the sentence although literally appropriate to the syntax. When Florent returns to Branchus' castle to give his answer to Branchus' grandmother, "forth sche cam, that olde Mone" (I, 1634) to hear the answer. "Mone" means "companion" or "old woman" depending on its etymology (see OED 1835), either of which fits the sentence. Given the context of the passage in which Florent "goth him forth with hevy chiere" (I, 1619) because he does not know how "he mai this worldes joie atteigne" (I, 1621), "mone" suggests the word "moan." The noun fits the sentence syntactically and alludes metonymically to Florent's mental state. Another sentence in which the pun fits the syntax literally but alludes to ideas of the tale is that in which Florent returns to the Loathly Lady, "and be the bridel sche him seseth" (I, 1697). The Loathly Lady seizes Florent's horse by the bridle, but since her intention is to marry Florent, the sentence suggests that she seizes him by the "bridall." The pun alludes to the theme of "forced marriage" (Glasser, 239) and calls attention to the situational humor and to the fact that the woman "tries to reverse the positions of the sexes" (Rowland, 248-49).[4]

Just as Gower shows the importance of the tales of Mundus and Paulina and of Florent in Book One in part by using numerous puns therein, so he shows that of other tales by the same rhetorical device. I should like to turn to the tale of Appolinus in Book Eight, because this long tale makes particularly vivid use of puns. Some of the puns are appropriate to both sense and syntax, as at the end of the tale when Appolinus has returned to Tyre and "hath take his *real* place" (VIII, 1902) [italics mine], an adjective which means both "real or actual" and "royal." Despite all his wanderings and disguises, Appolinus is actually a king, and his "real" place is therefore the "royal" place in the palace of Tyre. Some of the puns are literally appropriate to the syntax but metonymically appropriate to the sense of the sentence. When the daughter of Artestrathes falls in love with Appolinus, it is because "love hath mad him a querele/ Ayein hire youthe freissh and frele" (VIII, 837-38). The literal meaning of "querele" in the sentence is "arrow," recalling the fact that the god of love is an archer who shoots arrows at those whom he wishes to make fall in love. "Querele" also suggests Middle English "quarele/querele" [quarrel] and reminds us that the god of love has a quarrel with those young people who have not yet fallen in love. Gower presumably uses the form "querele" in this passage to evoke the pun because he elsewhere uses the form "quarel" to mean "arrow" or "bolt" (see V, 7239, for example).

In another passage in the tale of Appolinus, Gower uses the kind of pun that he uses on "beste" in the tale of Mundus and Paulina, in which two sentences, each of which permits only one meaning of a word to fit the syntax and the sense, form a metonymic web of allusions that make us think of the punning meanings of the word in the context of the whole passage. When Appolinus gives wheat to the Tharsians, "hath he noght his yifte *spilt*" (VIII, 570) [italics mine], and "spilt" means "wasted." While he is in Tharse, he receives the news that Antiochus "awaiteth if he mihte him *spille*" (VIII, 579) [italics mine], and in this line, "spille" means "destroy." The proximity of the two lines reminds us of the multiple meanings of the word in the context of the whole passage, and the two uses of the verb in its transitive sense remind us of the intransitive meaning "perish" or "fail." Because the tale of Appolinus explores such questions as the waste of human life and the failure of human endeavor, the multiple meanings of the verb are evoked in this passage.

Just as Gower uses puns to reinforce themes of particular tales, in a number of places in the frame story of the *Confessio*, he uses puns that are appropriate to their immediate context. In Book One, Amans is "wepinge" (I, 115) because of his failure as a lover, and he speaks of Venus, "that is the Source and *Welle*/ Of *wel* or wo" (I, 148-49) [italics mine], and asks her for "some *wele*" (I, 171) [italics mine] after his "longe wo" (I, 171). The close juxtaposition of "welle" [well] and "wel" [weal], especially in a context that emphasizes Amans' tears of "wo," also reminds us of the fountain that is always found in the *locus amoenus* of the love garden and the streams of grace found in poems like the *Divina Commedia* and *Pearl*. In Book Three, Amans says, "Betwen Danger and me/ Is evere *werre* til he deye" (III, 1564-65) [italics mine], and "werre" suggests both the literal meaning "war" and the metonymic meaning "worse." It implies that the "war" between Amans and the lady's Danger grows "worse." The pun is reinforced shortly thereafter with a couplet using a rhyme that puns on the two meanings of "werre": "Who mai to love make a werre,/ That he ne hath himself the werre?" (III, 1645-46). Since Gower uses the form "werse" (see III, 1563, for example) in some places in the *Confessio*, he presumably chooses "werre" in ll. 1565 and 1646 specifically to evoke the pun. In Book

One, Amans says that he writes poetry to his lady, including "caroles with ... wordes *qweinte*" (I, 2730) [italics mine], and in Book Eight, he sees that the pairs of lovers in the lover's paradise "the more *queinte* it made/ For love" (VIII, 2687-88) [italics mine]. In both passages, all the meanings of "qweinte/queinte" ("curious," "wise," "ingenious" "crafty," "gentle," and "highly elegant or refined") fit. In addition, given Gower's friendship with Chaucer and Amans' concern to seduce his lady, a modern reader wonders if the word recalls the Wife of Bath's use of "queynte" to refer to the female sexual organs (see Chaucer, 80: 444).

In many places in the *Confessio*, Gower uses puns appropriate to their immediate context but which are not part of a larger pattern of allusion. Describing the Zodiac, he says that Taurus is "with sterres set" (VII, 1021) so that "is he noght there sterreles" (VII, 1024) and that Scorpio also "is ... noght sterreles" (VII, 1126). Although the principle meaning of "sterreles" is "star-less" or "without stars," the lines suggest a pun on "stiereles" [without a rudder], especially appropriate because the stars are used to guide navigation. They also guide human conduct, and "the stat of realmes and of kinges/ .../ It is conceived of the Sterre" (VII, 646-48), the rudder that guides the "realmes."

Some puns suggest allusions to other puns in the *Confessio* although they do not form a web of major importance. In the tale of Constance, for example, the description of Constance's death says that "the god hath made of hire an ende,/ And fro this worldes *faierie*/ Hath take hire into compaignie" (II, 1592-94) [italics mine]. "Faierie" suggests magical power of an illusory kind, a power that can destroy the human soul that loves earthly things too much. It also reminds us that the world has power over us specifically because it is "fair" [beautiful] and recalls the line in the Prologue that says "al is bot a chirie *feire*" (Pro., 454) [italics mine]. The pun gains resonance from its use in other Middle English works; at the end of *Troilus and Criseyde*, Chaucer bids his audience, "Thynketh al nys but a faire/ This world, that passeth soone as floures faire" (479: 1840-41).

Many puns in the *Confessio* are appropriate to their context in a tale but also make allusions to other contexts, especially that of the sin which governs the book in which the tale is found. One such pun occurs in the tale of Namplus, which describes how the Greek fleet sails homeward from Troy. A "rage of gret tempeste hem hente" (III, 982), and the "rage" [fury as of wind or the sea] of the literal tempest turns into the "rage" [violent anger or violent action] of the metaphorical tempest that Namplus unleashes on the fleet in vengeance for the death of his son "Palamedes" (III, 1007). Since "Wrathe" (III, 21) is the sin that governs Book Three, the pun alludes to the subject of the book. Another example of such a pun occurs in the tale of Canace and Machaire. Canace writes to Machaire, "If that my litel *Sone deie*,/ Let him be beried in my grave" (III, 292-93) [italics mine], and shortly thereafter writes, "Fare wel, for I schal *sone deie*" (III, 305) [italics mine]. The pun on "Sone" [son] and "sone" [soon] underscores the sorrow that Gower expresses for the child who dies prematurely because of the cruelty of his grandfather.

A third example of a pun that alludes to a context larger than the immediate tale is found in a pun on "son" and "sun" in the tales of Phaeton and of Icarus. The former begins by speaking of "Phebus, which is the Sonne hote" (IV, 979). Like the pun on "Sone deie"/ "sone deie" in the tale of Canace and Machaire, this pun involves more than one word in the sentence, because the line can be translated as either "Phebus, who is the hot sun" or "Phebus, who is called the son" because he is the son of Jupiter. The pun on "sun" and "son" is an appropriate introduction for the tale of Phaeton; he is the "Sone" (IV, 982) of the sun who causes the world to burn with too much heat when he takes "into governance/ The Sonnes carte" (IV, 1008-9) and makes it the "son's cart." The tale which immediately follows the tale of Phaeton, that of Icarus, also deals with a son who disobeys his father's commands and gets into trouble because of the sun. Icarus, being a bad son, does not follow the advice "which his fader tawhte" (IV, 1063) him, and he flies "til that the Sonne his wynges cawhte" (IV, 1064) and he is killed.

The pun on "sun" and "son" also evokes the pun on "son" and "soon" because Phaeton and Icarus act rashly and do things too soon. The pun on "sone" thus helps make all three tales exemplars of the sin "cleped Negligence" (IV, 889), the "Secretaire" (IV, 888) of Sloth, and it is appropriate both to the tales themselves and to the larger context of Book Four as a whole. Near the beginning of Book Four, Gower says that "*Slowthe* is mihti to confounde/ The *spied* of every mannes werk" (IV, 300-1) [italics mine]. The primary meaning of the sentence is that the deadly sin of Sloth prevents success in human endeavors, but it suggests that the "slowness" associated with Sloth by authors like Langland, who speaks of "*Sleuthe* so *slow*" in B, XIII: 408 (see Ryan, *Langland* 136) [italics Ryan's], contrasts to the "speed" which may bring about success. Amans links Sloth with slowness when he says that his "tunge is slowh to crave" (IV, 54), an idea that Genius reiterates when he says that the man guilty of "Pusillamite" (IV, 314) "him lacketh bothe word and dede,/ Whereof he scholde his cause *spede*" (IV, 323-24) [italics mine], that is, succeed as quickly as possible in obtaining his "cause."

In one passage in which Gower discusses the branch of Sloth "which cleped is Foryetelnesse" (IV, 541), he uses puns that are not fully homphonous in order to form a web of allusions to the sin of Sloth which governs Book Four:

    And thus I stonde and thenke al one

> Of thing that helpeth ofte *noght*;
> Bot what I hadde afore thoght
> To speke, whanne I come there,
> It is foryete, as *noght* ne were,
> And stonde amased and assoted,
> That of *nothing* which I have *noted*
> I can *noght* thanne a *note* singe.
> . . . .
> For love his grace wol *noght* sende
> To that man which dar axe *non*.
> . . . .
> And what a man that foryet himselve,
> Among a thousand be *noght* tuelve,
> That wol him take in remembrance,
> Bot lete him falle and take his chaunce.
> (IV, 692-722) [italics mine]

The pun involving "noght," "nothing," the noun "note" [musical note], and the verb "note" [to take note] in close proximity to the particle "non" relates to the theme of Sloth in Book Four by emphasizing the need for spiritual alertness, activity, and harmony.

Some of the most intriguing puns in the *Confessio* are those which allude to themes like the Sea Voyage that run throughout the poem. The pun on "wise" [wise] and "wise" [manner] introduced in the tale of Nebuchadnezzar's Dream in the Prologue is found throughout the *Confessio*. In the tale of the Trump of Death, the family of the king's brother goes to beg mercy "in such a wise" (I, 2177) as may make the king merciful, that is, in a wise manner. The emperor Constantine, who shows his wisdom by practicing mercy and who receives a vision from God, sends his men to find Pope Silvester, and "in such a *wise* as he hem telleth/ The Mont wher that Silvestre duelleth/ Thei have in alle haste soght" (II, 3377-79) [italics mine], and "wise" suggests the wise manner in which the emperor recounts his dream. Ironically, Constantine's faith leads him to donate lands to the Church, a donation which "hath ... proved other wise" (II, 3484) than he intended, that is, he made the donation in an unwise way. The pun is also used ironically when Amans confesses to having committed the sin of "Cheste" (III, 510) and says that he has spoken in a manner that lacks wisdom: "Yit spak I word in such a wise" (III, 509). The ironic uses of the pun are only possible because of the many contexts in which it appears with no ironic intent.

Throughout the *Confessio*, Genius is trying to impart knowledge to Amans and make him wise. Another pun that continues Gower's exploration of the subject of the necessity for wisdom and virtuous action is one of the puns which "are phonetic similitudes" (Nash, 139) rather than fully homophonous puns. It is a pun on "wit" [the faculty of thinking or understanding] and "wyht" [a human being], and Langland uses the pun in *Piers Plowman* A, XI: 122: "That eche *wy3t* beo in *wil* his *wit* the to schewe" (see Ryan, *Langland* 134) [italics Ryan's]. Since human beings are characterized by their ability to think, understand, and reason, and since the process of confession involves this ability, the pun is relevant to the *Confessio* as a whole. When Genius and Amans explore Amans' guilt in respect to "Contek and Homicide" (III, 1093), Amans says, "Whan I my wittes overwende,/ Min hertes contek hath non ende" (III, 1131-32); one who "overwendes" his own "wittes" turns out to be behaving in a way unbecoming to a "wyht." Somewhat later in the same speech, Amans says that if a man "mote/ His oghne rewle have upon honde,/ Ther schal no witt ben understonde" (III, 1168-70). The pun on "witt" in l. 1170 suggests that a person's failure of understanding in his "wit" is related to a willful failure to understand another "wyht." The same pun occurs even more clearly in the description of Ulysses' prophetic dream about Thelogonus than it does in the passage about "Contek." In his dream, "Uluxes tho began to preie/ That this figure wolde him seie/ What *wyht* he is that seith him so./ This *wyht* upon a spere tho/ A pensel which was wel begon,/ Embrouded, scheweth him anon" (VI, 1549-54) [italics mine]. Ulysses then "preith to *wite* in some partie/ What thing it myhte signefie,/ 'A signe it is,' the *wyht* ansuerde,/ 'Of an Empire'" (VI, 1559-62) [italics mine]. Because Ulysses does not "wite" what "wyht" the sign betokens, he acts in a manner that causes his death, a fact that emphasizes the necessity for human beings to understand matters properly.

One theme that runs through the *Confessio* is that of the fire of love, introduced when the god of love throws "a firy Dart" (I, 144) at Amans and explored in numerous tales. One pun that reinforces this theme is that on "hote" [is called] and "hote" [hot] which is found in the line "Phebus, which is the Sonne hote" (IV, 979) discussed above. It is also found in a punning rhyme in the tale of Acis and Galatea, which speaks of "this yonge knyht [that] Acis was hote/ Which hire ayeinward als so hote/ Al only loveth and nomo" (II, 131-33).

The pun is used as part of a web in the *Confessio* that involves heat, burning, and the hell in which lovers often live when they are excluded from the lover's paradise. Amans says about his love for the unresponsive lady, "Ethna, which brenneth yer be yere,/ Was thanne noght so *hot* as I" (II, 20-21) [italics mine], naming himself metonymically as a "hot" lover whose "hertes thoght withinne brenneth" (II, 23). The fire of love that burns within Amans is analogous to that within Poliphemus; the love between Acis and Galatea "al his herte hath set afyre/ Of pure Envie: and as a fyre" (II, 149-50) he goes mad because of love. As a result, "he ran Ethna the *hell* aboute,/ Wher nevere yit the fyr was oute" (II, 163-64) [italics mine]. The fire of the volcano externalizes the fire of Envy in his heart that causes him to slay Acis "with falling of this hell" (II, 176). The meaning of "hell" that is literal to both the sense and the syntax of the passage is "hill," but the volcanic fires suggest a punning meaning literal to the syntax and metonymically appropriate to the sense of the passage, that of "hell." The pun of "hill" and "hell" is reinforced by its presence in other passages, as in the tale of Ceïx and Alceone, in which "the god of Slep" (IV, 2989) lives in a house located where "under an *hell* ther is a Cave" (IV, 2991) [italics mine]. The cave is literally under a "hill," but since it is located in Hell, the meaning "hell" is appropriate to the line. Since Gower also uses the variant spelling "hull," as in the tale of Gideon, in which a "Sarazin" (VII, 3702) dreams of "a barli cake,/ Which fro the Hull his weie hath take" (VII, 3705-6), I should like to suggest that when he uses "hell," he wants to remind us of the pun of "hill" and "hell."

The fire with which Amans and Poliphemus burn and which makes them live in a hellish state is that of sexual desire. The *Confessio* puns on "lust" to explore the meanings "pleasure," "delight," "a source of pleasure or delight," and "sexual appetite." "Cheste" (III, 417) is a sin "which many a lusti love hath twinned" (III, 423); "lusti" means "pleasurable," "giving pleasure," and "concupiscent," and, according to Genius, "love upon his lust wakende/ Is evere" (IV, 3181-82), implying by the pun on "lust" that love is intent on pleasure, specifically, on sexual pleasure. The pun on "lust" is one of a number of puns in a passage about the knighthood of King David:

> Knyhthode he kepte in such a *wise*,
> That for no fleisshli covoitise
> Of *lust* to ligge in ladi *armes*
> He lefte noght the *lust* of *armes*.
> For where a Prince hise *lustes suieth*
> That he the werre noght *poursuieth*,
> Whan it is time to ben *armed*,
> His contre stant fulofte harmed.
> (VII, 4347-54) [italics mine]

The puns on "lust" and "armes," coupled with the punning rhyme of "suieth" and "poursuieth," makes a contrast between the pleasure that a knight takes in armed conflict during war and that which he takes in sexual pleasure "in ladi armes" (VII, 4349), suggesting that the latter can impede the former and that one who acts in a wise "wise" (VII, 4347) is cognizant of the fact. The two forms of "lust" can be compatible when a man pursues them with the proper understanding, for in his vision of the lover's paradise, Amans sees those whose "speche/ Was al of knyhthod and of *Armes*,/ And what it is to ligge in *armes*/ With love" (VIII, 2496-99) [italics mine]. As in the case of many points in the *Confessio*, the compatibility of the two uses of "armes" depends on understanding, wisdom, and moderation.

According to Kenneth Muir, puns "make the listener aware of a complex of ideas which enrich the total statement, even though they do not come into full consciousness" ("Uncomic Pun" 483). By this statement about puns, Muir helps us understand how puns work in the *Confessio*. The study of puns in the *Confessio* inevitably leads to a study of Gower's use of puns for the rhyming elements of couplets, as he does in the rhyme of "armes" (VII, 4349, and VIII, 2498) [human arms] and "armes" (VII, 4350, and VIII, 2497) [armaments]. I have deferred a discussion of the punning rhymes to a separate chapter because they present problems different from those presented by other puns.[5]

Chapter Four

Linguistics and Literary Structure: Metonymy and the *Confessio Amantis*

Gower's puns in the *Confessio Amantis* allude metonymically to key ideas and themes and are a serious part of his poetic technique. His technique is not exclusively metonymic because of the nature of his chosen form, octosyllabic couplets. Jakobson has argued that "the metrical parallelism of lines or the phonic equivalence of rhyming words" means that poetry is by nature metaphoric and that "there exist ... grammatical and anti-grammatical but never agrammatical rhymes" (127). Much of the *Confessio* exhibits metrical parallelism and the phonic equivalence of rhymes, and it therefore partakes of the metaphoric structure of language and poetry. Nevertheless, not all rhymes in medieval poetry show semantic similarity in the same way that rhymes do in more modern poetry. Instead, some show contiguity because they derive from an oral-formulaic structure in which the rhymes must be "systematic" (see Quinn-Hall, 111) [italics deleted] and predictable rather than merely "conventional" (see Quinn-Hall, 111) [italics deleted]. The techniques of oral-formulaic poetry tend to be metonymic rather than metaphoric.

When one studies the works of fourteenth-century poets who, in contrast to the *jongleurs*, composed in writing rather than improvising orally, one finds it difficult to determine whether particular rhymes are conventional and therefore metonymic or chosen for rhetorical effect and therefore metaphoric. Walter S. Phelan observes that the frequency of "late" and "algate" in the *Confessio* is caused by "their use as a rhyming pair" (478), an example of "words whose frequency seems to be due to a readiness for rhyming" (466) and which are therefore conventional rhymes. In contrast, William A. Quinn and Audley S. Hall provide extensive tables of the "*systematic* and *common*" (102) [italics Quinn-Hall's] end-rhymes of *King Horn*, including "rewe"/"trewe" (see 103) and "rewþe"/"trewþe" (see 144 and 146). These tables show that such rhymes are not conventional but assist the *jongleur* in performance because of metonymic association. Myra Stokes has argued that Chaucer's frequent use of rhyming words (including "rewe"/"trewe" and "routhe"/"trouthe") is such that "these rhyming 'formulas' ... play an important part in reflecting the meaning of the poem as it evolves" ("Recurring Rhymes" 287) and highlighting themes.

Although a statistical analysis of the rhymes of the *Confessio* is not the purpose of this study, I should like to point out that Gower, like Chaucer, sometimes uses rhymes used formulaically by earlier oral poets, but he uses them with rhetorical purpose. Book One, for example, is concerned with truth in love, and Gower exploits the imagery of the meanings of "routhe" [pity] and "trouthe" [truth], calling attention thereto in a passage in which the words rhyme:

> And riht so if a womman chese
> Upon the wordes that sche hiereth
> Som man, whan he most *trewe* appiereth,
> Thanne is he forthest fro the *trowthe*;
> Bot yit fulofte, and that is *rowthe*,
> Thei speden that ben most *untrewe*,
> And loven every day a newe,
> Whereof the lief is after loth
> And love hath cause to be wroth.
> (I, 1196-1204) [italics mine]

In this passage, the rhyme of "trowthe" and "rowthe," although conventional as is the rhyme in *Troilus and Criseyde*, is clearly deliberately chosen and is not therefore systematic as is the same rhyme in *King Horn*. It operates metaphorically rather than metonymically.

In some cases, Gower uses rhymes that are metonymic rather than metaphoric, for he frequently uses a common medieval poetic device which Burrow calls a "clever, difficult rhyme" (*Ricardian Poetry* 20) and which is known as "rime équivoque" (see Langlois, 442-43), "rime riche" (see Kökeritz and Ito, "Gower's Use" and *John Gower*, 214-31), or "identical rhyme" (see Robinson's note on the subject, Chaucer, 651).[1] An example of Gower's use of "rime équivoque" occurs when Amans tells Genius, "If that I dore,/ Er I come fulli to the Dore,/ I torne ayein and feign a thing" (IV, 2825-27). The rhyme of "dore" and "Dore" emphasizes Amans' diffidence in respect to his lady, which results in his exclusion from her company when he leaves by the "Dore."

Helge Kökeritz observes that "in medieval poetics the linking in rhyme of two homonyms or of the same word in different senses was considered a tour de force and was widely practiced" (945). Kate Harris has noted, however, that medieval editors sometimes viewed "rime équivoque" with distaste, sometimes rewriting or omitting the couplets and "excising such forms almost completely" (38). Gower's use of "rime équivoque" is a deliberate poetic device which we should study as part of his literary artistry. As Burrow observes, however, the typical modern reader "does not usually enjoy punning rhymes" (*Ricardian Poetry* 21), and their use in Middle English poetry and particularly in that of Gower has been little discussed. Gower's extensive use of "rime équivoque" is related to his use of puns (see Ito, *John Gower* 236), and, like puns, "rime équivoque" underscores what Muir calls "the logical sequence of thought" (Muir, "Uncomic Pun" 483). Because puns depend on contiguity for their effect, Gower's use of "rime équivoque" is metonymic rather than metaphoric.

In his study of Gower's use of "rime équivoque," Ito tabulates the use of such rhymes by both Gower and Chaucer. He shows that Chaucer uses 192 in 35,808 lines of poetry, a frequency of .54% (see *John Gower* 230), whereas Gower uses 383 in the 33,408 lines of the *Confessio* and 241 in the 21,450 lines of the *Mirour*, in each case a frequency of 1.1% (see *John Gower* 215). The frequency in both poems permits us to consider "rime équivoque" an important aspect of Gower's poetic technique, especially since the percentage would be higher if we included another form of punning rhyme not counted by Ito, the "quasi" (*John Gower* 225) "rime équivoque" like the rhyme of "worldesriche" (V, 87) with "riche" (V, 88).

Ito shows that Gower uses two sub-classes of "rime équivoque," the "S(emantic)-type," which links "two homophonous but semantically different words" and which provides "an interplay between verbal sound and verbal sense" (*John Gower* 220), and the "G(rammatical)-type," which consists of "two words which are different not semantically but grammatically only (e.g., *love*(n.): *love*(v.)" (*John Gower* 222) [italics Ito's]. The latter, which comprise only one-fourth of Gower's "rimes équivoques" (see Ito, *John Gower* 222), are especially interesting because they demonstrate, in contrast to Jakobson's assertion, that some rhymes can be "agrammatical" (127). Ito considers that Gower's use of "rime équivoque" exemplifies the rhetorical devices of "*traductio*" and "*annominatio*," whose "essential nature" is "the repetition of verbal sound" (*John Gower* 247) [italics Ito's]. His study is an example of the kind of historical scholarship that suggests that Gower uses poetic devices acceptable in the Middle Ages but not in the twentieth century. The analysis of the rhymes as metonymic structures makes a similar point from the point of view of linguistics rather than medieval rhetoric.

A careful survey of Gower's use of rhymes shows that he uses "rime équivoque" deliberately rather than because a particular rhyme is systematic and predictable in a particular place. Ito calls attention to the fact that "cluster" (*John Gower* 225) "rimes équivoques," that is, a series of couplets up to twelve lines in length each of which is a "rime équivoque," like that in Book One, ll. 2905-10, usually occur, not in the tales, but in the dialogues between Genius and Amans or in the speeches "to the reader [spoken] by Gower as narrator or preacher" (*John Gower* 225). This fact suggests that Gower uses "rime équivoque" with conscious literary artistry as part of his devices to call attention to particular points. For example, near the beginning of Book Five, there is a cluster ten lines long which refers to avaricious love and uses "rimes équivoques" to underscore the point:

> And in this wise, taketh *kepe*,
> If I hire hadde, I wolde hire *kepe*,

> And yit no friday wolde I *faste*,
> Thogh I hire kepte and hielde *faste*.
> Fy on the bagges in the *kiste*!
> I hadde ynogh, if I hire *kiste*.
> For certes, if sche were *myn*,
> I hadde hir levere than a *Myn*
> Of Gold; for al this *worldesriche*
> Ne mihte make me so *riche*
> As sche, that is so inly *good*.
> I sette noght of other *good*.
> (V, 79-90) [italics mine]

Amans reinforces the ideas in this passage when he says, "Thus I wolde/ Ben averous, if that I scholde" (V, 97-98), linking the sin of avarice to the theme of the improper use of love by the use of the words "kiste" [chest], "Myn" [mine], "riche" [rich], and "good" [goods]. It should be noted that Langland also uses the pun on the virtue "good" and "good" [goods] in *Piers Plowman* (see Ryan, *Langland* 134).

An extended example of the rhetorical effectiveness of the repeated use of a particular "rime équivoque" occurs in Book One, in which Gower rhymes "understonde" (ll. 287, 306, 564, 2262, 2908, and 3445) with "stonde" (ll. 288, 305, 563, 2261, 2907, and 3446). The fact that the rhyme occurs in the final couplet (ll. 3445 and 3446) of Book One calls attention to its importance. Gower uses this rhyme frequently in the *Confessio*; in Book Eight, Venus tells Amans, "Thou most as of thi love stonde/ For I thi bille have understonde" (VIII, 2323-24). By the rhyme, Gower emphasizes the importance of a proper understanding of virtue and vice as the basis for proper action and links it to the idea of standing (both physically and morally) with rectitude. He calls attention to this idea in Book One because five of the rhymes occur in the dialogue between Genius and Amans and only one in an encapsulated narrative, in the story of Daniel's sermon to Nebuchadnezzar, an analogous situation because the rhyme occurs in a dialogue. Gower does not, however, always rhyme "understonde" with "stonde." In the tale of the Three Questions, the maiden tells her father, "Let me go with you to the king,/ And ye schull make him understonde/ How ye, my wittes forto fonde,/ Have leid your ansuere upon me" (I, 3196-99). The alternation of "rime équivoque" with rhymes like "understonde"/"fonde" shows that Gower chooses his rhymes to suit the meaning of a passage and therefore uses "rime équivoque" to call attention to particular ideas.

"Rime équivoque," like puns generally, calls attention to the links between two concepts which appear to be different, forcing us to focus on underlying similarities beneath surface differences. Gower uses "rime équivoque" as one technique to call attention to the relationship between concepts. The tale of Florent in Book One has received much critical attention because it is an analogue of Chaucer's *Wife of Bath's Tale.* As Olga C. M. Fischer notes, the versions differ mainly because of Gower's and Chaucer's "adaptation[s] of the tale to the respective narrators, ... whose motives for telling the tale are of a rather different nature" (205). Although the tale of Florent is "simply told" (Peck, 46), Gower uses eighteen examples of "rime équivoque" to highlight its points and reinforce other rhetorical devices like repetition of key words (see Phelan). Gower's use of "rime équivoque" helps to reinforce associations and clarify ideas.

Gallacher has discussed the tale of Florent in its narrative context ("Murmur and Compleignte" [l, 1345]), pointing out that "Florent must obey the implications of his own verbal agreement" (88) at each stage of the story, a fact that Gower emphasizes by "frequent references to Florent's 'trowthe'" (88). In an analogous study, Phelan presents in tabular form "a frequency vocabulary" (464) of the tale of Florent in comparison with the *Wife of Bath's Tale* and selected other tales by Gower. Although he notes that frequency of a word alone "has no direct correlation with its thematic or structural importance" (464), he shows that a study of repetitions can identify the associations made by a poet's semantic usages. From his study, one can understand the nature of Gower's associative use of repeated terminology and concepts.

The repeated concepts are further highlighted by Gower's use of "rime équivoque." Gower calls attention to the theme of "trowthe" in Genius' introduction to the tale: "Toward this vice of which we trete/ Ther ben yit tweie of thilke estrete ..." (I, 1343-44). The importance of speech is emphasized in the tale by the use of a "rime équivoque" in the speech of Branchus' "grantdame" (I, 1445): "Thou unto a questioun/ Which I schal axe schalt ansuere:/ And over this thou schalt ek swere ..." (I, 1460-62). Both of these couplets are examples of "quasi" "rime équivoque," for each rhymes a simplex with a compound derived therefrom.

The most important use of "rime équivoque" to underscore the theme of speech is an example of what Ito calls the grammatical type and which I have argued is the best example of metonymic "rime équivoque." At the turning point of the tale, Florent promises the "olde wyht" (I, 1548), "Have hier myn hond, I schal thee wedde" (I, 1587), which rhymes with Genius' assertion, "And thus his trowthe he leith to wedde" (I, 1588). "Wedde" in l. 1588 is a noun meaning a promise or a covenant; "wedde" in l. 1587 is a verb with the specific meaning of contracting a marriage covenant. Gower uses "wedde" as a simple pun in l. 1770 (see discussion in chapter three), and he uses it in a "rime équivoque" in the tale of the False Bachelor: "He seith, the kinges Dowhter wedde,/ For so the Ring was leid to wedde" (II, 2661-62). In both tales, this "rime équivoque" that rhymes two words that differ grammatically alludes metonymically to the important themes of "trowthe" and the ethical use of speech. It should be noted that Gower does not choose this particular "rime équivoque" because of lack of adequate rhyming vocabulary; in the *Confessio*, "wedde" can, for example, rhyme with "spedde" (see II, 623-24). Gower must, therefore, have chosen this rhyme for its effect.

Many of the "rimes équivoques" in the tale of Florent are of the "quasi" variety. Some rhyme either a word and a derivative thereof ("undertake"/"take," I, 1485-86) or two words compounded from the same root ("vengement"/"juggement," I, 1457-58; "receive"/"deceive," I, 1465-66; and "opposed"/"supposed," I, 1649-50). Like the grammatical-type "rime équivoque," these rhymes are contiguous and therefore metonymic, for they form an associative pattern that alludes to important themes in the tale. The importance of covenants in the tale of Florent is underscored when Genius says, "Florent this thing hath undertake,/ The day was set, the time take" (I, 1485-86).

Other examples of "quasi" "rime équivoque" rhyme words which are phonologically identical only in their last syllables and are like Ito's category of semantic-type rhymes, although they are not etymologically related ("disposicioun"/"complexioun," I, 1497-98; "leve"/"beleve," I, 1515-16; "mene"/"bemene," I, 1539-40; "avised"/"devised," I, 1543-44; "lefte"/"uplefte," I, 1673-74; and "aweie"/"weie," I, 1711-12). Because they associate ideas that are in no way similar, such rhymes are metonymic. They underscore themes of the tale, as, for example, the theme of truth and covenant when the "olde wyht" (I, 1548) warns Florent, "Thou hast on honde such a game,/ That bot thou be the betre avised,/ Thi deth is schapen and devised,/ .../ Bot if that thou my conseil have" (I, 1542-46).

The way in which the associative links work may be exemplified by the lines in which Florent grieves that "his youthe schal be cast aweie/ Upon such on which as the weie/ Is old and lothly overal" (I, 1711-13). His loss of his hopes of happiness is emphasized by the rhyme of "aweie," a word which suggests where his hopes have gone, and "weie" [whey], with an additional pun on "weie" [way]. The use of "way" as an image of worthlessness reminds us of Conscience's comment in *Piers Plowman* that Mede is "as commune as the cartwey" (Langland, 28: III: 132). Florent's loss turns to gain because he yields to necessity ("nede he mot that nede schal" [I, 1714]) and behaves "for pure gentilesse" (I, 1721), letting his wife choose what is best for them both. Similar uses of "rime équivoque" occur in the frame story. For example, Amans tells Genius, "Whan so is that I se and hiere/ Or hevy word or hevy chiere/ Of my lady, I grucche *anon*;/ Bot wordes dar I speke *non*" (I, 1383-86) [italics mine]. The rhyme calls attention to the point he is making, that although he is not guilty of "Murmur and Compleignte of love" (I, 1378) in his speech, he is guilty of it in his "herte" (I, 1388). He is therefore guilty of "unbuxomnesse" (I, 1394), a major theme of Book One.

The above discussion of Book One of the *Confessio* has shown the importance of understanding Gower's use of metonymy in order to understand his poetic artistry. Such an understanding helps us to appreciate other sections of the *Confessio* as well. Macaulay argues that the least effective narrative is the tale of Appolinus. Although he attributes what he perceives as lack of artistry to the fact that the tale "was in its original form so loose and rambling a series of incidents, that hardly any skill could have completely redeemed it" (Gower, vol. I: xii), I believe that his lack of sympathy derives from the fact that he does not understand the metonymic nature of the tale. Because he underrates the poetic artistry of the tale, he also underrates its narrative artistry. Although recent critics (see, for example, Goodall and Goolden, "Antiochus's Riddle") have studied the narrative and shown its excellence, no-one has studied its poetic artistry in detail. In this chapter, I wish to discuss Gower's use of details like "rime équivoque" and allusive language; in chapter five, I will discuss his adaptation of a larger rhetorical pattern that functions metonymically, a type-scene from the vernacular formulaic tradition.

Peck argues that a major theme of Book Eight is "the rediscovery of right relationships" (161) with a special emphasis on the "motif of 'kynde'" (163), and he suggests that the tale of Appolinus is appropriate for the conclusion of the *Confessio* because it ties together the themes of the poem. Gower has written the tale of Appolinus in such a way that the poetry underscores the themes. This fact is particularly apparent when we compare the tale to a poetic "Cronique in daies gon" (VIII, 271), the twelfth-century *Pantheon* by Gotfried von Viterbo, which Gower claims for his source even though he, as Macaulay has shown, "unquestionably followed mainly the Latin prose narrative which was commonly current" (Gower, vol. II: 537).[2] G. A. A. Kortekaas observes that the *Pantheon* is composed of "two generally rhyming hexameters followed by one pentameter" (152). An example of the normal kind of stanza is the first; the terminal words of the lines are "decore," "amore," and "dolet" (Gotfried, 153: 1-3). Occasionally, all three lines rhyme, as in the twenty-third stanza, whose lines end with the words "potiri," "iniri," and "viri" (Gotfried, 155: 67-69). Numerous lines rhyme internally; for example, in the first line of stanza eleven, the word before the caesura, "plangit," rhymes with the last word of the line, "tangit" (Gotfried, 154: 31-33). Normally, a stanza forms a single syntactical unit, and the narrative is spare and unadorned. Kortekaas comments that the *Pantheon* is most noteworthy because the author revised several times, "because he tried to smooth out certain unevennesses and improbabilities in the original tale, and because he endeavored to lift the story out of the ambiance of the fairy-tale by placing the protagonist Apollonius historically towards the end of the Punic wars" (152) rather than because of its poetic artistry. Despite the care with which Gotfried revised his poem, it shows no signs of the metonymic artistry which characterizes Gower's tale with its evocative language and use of "rime équivoque."

In a number of instances, Gower uses "rimes équivoques" that he uses throughout the *Confessio* in order to emphasize themes of importance in the entire work, although his emphasis differs in this tale to accord with the themes in question. For example, throughout the *Confessio* Gower uses the rhyme of "stand" and "understand" to emphasize the idea that a person must understand virtue and stand with rectitude. In Book One, he normally uses it in the dialogue between Genius and Amans, but in Book Eight, he uses it, not only in the frame story (VIII, 2029 and 2030, for example), but also in the tale of Appolinus, rhyming "stonde" (VIII, 647 and 1509) with "understonde" (VIII, 648 and 1510) twice and "stod" (VIII, 355 and 905) with "understod" (VIII, 356 and 906) twice. The princes who court Antiochus' daughter "knew nothing hou it stod" (VIII, 355) between father and daughter, and when Antiochus "understod" (VIII, 356) that his daughter had suitors, he concocted a plot to keep her for himself. The result is that the princes' lack of understanding brings about their deaths.

The second rhyme of "stod" and "understod" occurs in the story of another father, Artestrathes, and his daughter, a story which, as Goodall observes, "reflects in a very interesting way on that between Antiochus and his daughter" (243). In the scene parallel to that in which the princes court Antiochus' daughter, "Princes Sones thre" (VIII, 867) ask to marry Artestrathes' daughter, but she writes a letter expressing her desire to marry Appolinus. The letter is brought "tofore the king, ther as he stod" (VIII, 905), and "whan that he it understod" (VIII, 906), he arranges for her to marry Appolinus. Goodall points out that the second scene is narratively the inverse of the first, but he does not note that the repetition of the rhyme of "stod" and "understod" makes a linguistic link between the two scenes.

In the third case, in which the rhyme of "stand" and "understand" is used, Gower says that when Appolinus has been shipwrecked on the shores of Pentapolim, "a Fisshere" (VIII, 646) "sih a man ther naked stonde,/ And whan that he hath understonde/ The cause, he hath of him gret routhe" (VIII, 647-49). Gower emphasizes the moral responsibility of everyone-- Amans, the characters in the tales, and the members of the audience--to have proper understanding and practice "routhe" towards others. With the last use of the rhyme in the tale, Gower provides the negative inverse of the theme to underscore it: Theophilus falsely reports to Dionise that he has slain Thaise and says, "kepe conseil, hou so it stonde" (VIII, 1509), to which Gower adds, "This fend, which this hath understonde,/ Was glad, and weneth it be soth" (VIII, 1510-11). The four uses of this particular "rime équivoque" relate to those which have gone before in the *Confessio*, forming a web of allusions that relates the tales, not just narratively, but also linguistically.

One of the most important examples of "rime équivoque" in the tale of Appolinus occurs in the riddle which Antiochus poses to his daughter's suitors, a riddle not found in Gotfried von Viterbo's version[3] so that one cannot compare Gower's poetic technique to that of Gotfried. It is noteworthy, however, that Gower has chosen to translate the Latin prose version of the riddle in such a way that he uses an example of "quasi" "rime équivoque" to call attention to the importance of the riddle linguistically. The lines in question are the opening of the riddle, "With felonie I am upbore,/ I ete and have it noght forbore/ Mi modres fleissh" (VIII, 405-7). The rhyme of "upbore" and "forbore," both derived from the verb "bere," alludes to several ideas in the portion of the tale devoted to Antiochus and his daughter. It alludes to the facts that "the wylde fader thus devoureth/ His oghne fleissh" (VIII, 309-10) rather than forbearing it and that the daughter "hath forlore/ The flour which sche hath longe bore" (VIII, 303-4). Most important, it alludes to the fact that the daughter becomes a willing participant in her father's sin and later shares his fate ("So be thei bothe in o balance" [VIII, 1002]) because she bears with evil and attributes her lack of moral decision to necessity: "So suffren thei that suffre mote" (VIII, 340).

This careful metonymic weaving of allusions using the verb "bere" both in the riddle and in the remainder of the story about Antiochus and his daughter shows Gower's poetic artistry and permits us to answer Peter Goolden's charge that Gower's version of the riddle merely translates the Latin so that he "wonders whether Gower did any more than reproduce the words themselves; whether he penetrated to the dark meaning underneath is open to conjecture" ("Antiochus's Riddle" 248). In contrast, I believe that an understanding of Gower's use of metonymy shows that he is indeed aware of the meaning of the riddle; moreover, he is aware of the relation thereof to themes he uses in other places in the *Confessio*. Although he does not rhyme "upbore" and "forbore" in other places, he uses "upbore" again in Book Eight, to describe Appolinus' shipwreck, when "a table" (VIII, 630) from the ship "to the land him hath upbore;/ The remenant was al forlore" (VIII, 631-32). These lines emphasize Appolinus' escape and remind us that he bears his sufferings with fortitude and a proper moral disposition. The only other use of the verb "upbore" in the *Confessio* occurs in Book Five, when Genius speaks of "the seintz that weren ous tofore,/ Be whom the feith was ferst upbore" (V, 1813-14). The use of "upbore" in the riddle emphasizes that Antiochus' behavior is the inverse, not only of that of Arthestrathes, but also of that of the virtuous Appolinus and the saints whom members of the audience should emulate. The unusual "rime équivoque" that introduces the riddle has been chosen to allude metonymically to an important didactic theme of the *Confessio*.

Another important use of "quasi" "rime équivoque" in the tale of Appolinus occurs just before the reunited family is about to depart from Ephesus: "Thei maden ther an ende,/ And token leve and gon to Schipe/ With al the hole felaschipe" (VIII, 1884-86). The rhyme of the literal word for a sea-going vessel ("Schipe") and the word "felaschipe" in which "-schipe" is a derivational morpheme is related to the simple pun Gower uses on the same word and morpheme. It alludes to two themes of the tale, the importance of proper relationships between people particularly shown by what Peck calls the "motif of 'kynde'" (163) and the type-scene of the Sea Voyage which embodies important themes of the *Confessio* (see chapter five).

The same rhyme occurs at other significant points in the *Confessio*, alluding to a real or metaphorical Sea Voyage. In Book One, for example, the Greeks leave Troy "with al the hole felaschipe,/ And forth thei wenten into Schipe" (I, 1163-64) after the Trojan Horse has been taken into Troy. Although their purpose and fellowship are fraudulent rather than morally good as are those of Appolinus and his family, and although the Sea Voyage is never really undertaken, the rhyme suggests the importance of "felaschipe" on the Sea Voyage of life. The point is underscored by the frequent use of the rhyme in the *Confessio*.

In other places, Gower rhymes words identical only in the derivational morpheme "-schipe," and he uses this morpheme meaning the quality or condition of the first element of the word deliberately, because he uses variant compounds. Although he uses "drunkenschipe" to rhyme with "felaschipe" (see the tale of Midas, V, 149-50, for example), he uses "drunkenesse" to rhyme with "witnesse" (see the tale of Galba and Vitellius, VI, 585-86, for example). In the tale of the Travellers and the Angel, Gower rhymes "kindeschipe" (II, 325) and "felaschipe" (II, 326), calling attention to the fact that good fellowship should be in accordance with the laws of "kinde." In the tale of Saul in Book Four, he rhymes "worschipe" (IV, 1957) and "felaschipe" (IV, 1958), showing that Jonathon's death in fellowship with his father is brought about by the father's pursuit of his own "worschipe." All four of these rhyming couplets form a network of allusions that link the derivational morpheme and the words with which it forms compounds to the idea that life is a voyage on stormy seas.

An intriguing variant of the normal use of "rime équivoque" in the tale of Appolinus involves the use of puns that are not "phonetic similitudes" (Nash, 139) because the words are not fully homophonous. Gower uses this kind of pun in the tale of Appolinus to link disparate concepts, and his rhymes of such words as "melodie" and "maladie" and "obeie" and "abeie" represent what Heller calls "partial identity of the manifesting units" (275). In the first example, when Appolinus flees from Tyre, the Tyrians have lost their "lust" (VIII, 476) and take "upon hem such penaunce" (VIII, 477) that "every mirth and melodie/ To hem was thanne a maladie" (VIII, 479-80). The allusive rhyme of "melodie" and "maladie" is not necessitated by the difficulty of finding a rhyme because "maladie" can rhyme with, for example, "Envie" (see II, 9-10). It is also found in the tale of Tereus, when Philomene, transformed into a nightingale, laments and "of loves maladie/ Sche makth diverse melodie" (V, 5991-92). In the tale of Tereus, the rhyme emphasizes the sorrow of Philomene; in that of Appolinus, it emphasizes that of the Tyrians. In the latter tale, music is of especial importance; as Gallacher points out, Artestrathes' daughter falls in love with Appolinus when "her sense of hearing is ravished by his musical skill" (132). The "rime équivoque" in ll. 479-80 prepares us both for the scene with Artestrathes' daughter and for that in which Thaise is sent with her harp to use both speech and "melodie" to heal Appolinus' "maladie." In the latter scene, Gower uses a true "rime équivoque" of the grammatical type to call attention to the theme of the use of music to heal, for Thaise "goth hir doun, ther as he lay,/ Wher that sche harpeth many a lay" (VIII, 1669-70) and talks to him until he puts "awey his hevy chiere" (VIII, 1701).

A second example of semi-homophonous "rime équivoque" occurs when Artestrathes' daughter falls in love and learns that "malgre wher sche wole or noght,/ Sche mot with al hire hertes thoght/ To love and to his lawe obeie;/ And that sche schal ful sore abeie" (VIII, 839-42). In the tale of Rosiphelee, the same rhyme occurs; "the wofull woman" (IV, 1351) laments, "Me liste noght to love obeie,/ And that I now ful sore abeie" (IV, 1389-90). In both cases, although "obeie" and "abeie" are not etymologically related, the similarity of sound suggests that obedience, an important theme of the *Confessio*, is related metonymically to what a person is willing to purchase.

The other two examples of semi-homophonous "rime équivoque" involve the presence or the absence of aspiration. This type of pun is to be expected in the bilingual environment of those speaking Anglo-Norman and English. A famous example of such a pun in Middle English occurs in Chaucer's *Summoner's Tale*; the friar's question, "What is a ferthyng worth parted in twelve?" (Chaucer, 96: 1967), provokes Thomas' revenge, so that "ferthyng" turns out to be a pun on "farthing" and "farting" (see Baum, "Chaucer's Puns: A Supplementary List" 167). An analogous pun occurs in *Piers Plowman*, when Holi Chirche says that "*feith* withouten *feet* is feblere than nought" (16: I: 186) [italics mine]. Since Chaucer and Langland use puns involving aspiration, it is appropriate to consider that Gower used similar puns and that the audience appreciated them. Gower rhymes "while" (VIII, 533) and "wyle" (VIII, 534)--a "rime équivoque" also found in Book Two, ll. 2475-76--and "whiel" (VIII, 1737) and "wel" (VIII, 1738). In the first case, the pun links the short time ("while") for which Antiochus regrets his inability to kill Appolinus with his wiliness. In the second case, the pun calls attention to the theme of Fortune's Wheel which is important in the tale (see Gallacher, 130-37) and in the *Confessio*: "Fortune hath sworn/ To sette him upward on the whiel;/ So goth the world, now wo, now wel" (VIII, 1736-38). For a member of an audience attuned to the way that Gower uses traditional images for literary effect, the use in Book Eight echoes a use in Book One which also alludes to the theme of Fortune's Wheel ("And natheles sche wiste wel,/ Mi world stod on an other whiel" [I, 177-78]).[4] Gower's infrequent use of such "rimes équivoques" suggests that he chose them purposefully for the associations they evoke.

In five cases in the tale of Appolinus, Gower uses "rimes équivoques" in what Ito calls clusters (see *John Gower* 225), unusual because he tends to use clusters in the narrative rather than in the tales. These five clusters, which in each case consist of two couplets, are especially important for the ideas and themes they evoke. In the first, the importance of the rhyme "stonde"/"understonde" is emphasized because it is the second couplet in a cluster: "Whanne him thoughte alle grace aweie;/ Ther cam a Fisshere in the weie,/ And sih a man ther naked stonde,/ And whan that he hath understonde/ The cause, he hath of him gret routhe" (VIII, 645-49). In both couplets, Gower rhymes a word and a compound derived therefrom, and the four lines emphasize the importance of proper relationships and the grace that God gives people.

Three more of the clusters occur during the narrative about the sojourn Appolinus makes in Pentapolim and the voyage during which his wife apparently dies. The four clusters call attention to the particular importance of this section in its exploration of proper relationships between fathers and daughters and the importance of Christian marriage and "right relationships" (Peck, 161) in general. King Artestrathes decrees that Appolinus "with al that evere he may/ This yonge faire freisshe May/ Of that he couthe scholde enforme;/ And full assented in this forme/ Thei token leve as for that nyht" (VIII, 815-19), making it possible for the princess to fall in love with Appolinus and marry him.

The fourth cluster, ll. 923-26, involves a couplet that rhymes "corage" (VIII, 923) and "mariage" (VIII, 924) and continues the theme of proper relationships. The last cluster in the important central section of the tale occurs when Appolinus grieves after his wife seems to have died in childbirth: "Was nevere man that sih ne wiste/ A sorwe unto his sorwe lich;/ For evere among upon the lich;/ He fell swoundende, as he that soghte/ His oghne deth, which he besoghte/ Unto the goddes alle above/ With many a pitous word of love" (VIII, 1074-80). This cluster calls attention to the end of the section dealing with Appolinus' "kinde" relationship with his wife and introduces the section of the poem that deals with the healthy relationship between Appolinus and his daughter, Thaise. This relationship teaches us "what is to be so sibb of blod" (VIII, 1703).

The last cluster of the tale occurs on the voyage in which "the hihe god" (VIII, 1789) tells Appolinus to travel to Ephesus rather than Tharse, the voyage which results in his reunion with his wife. "Withoute lette of eny wente/ With Seil updrawe forth thei wente/ Towards Tharse upon the tyde./ Bot he that wot what schal betide,/ The hihe god, which wolde him kepe,/ Whan that this king was faste aslepe,/ Be nyhtes time he hath him bede/ To seile into an other stede:/ To Ephesim he bad him drawe" (VIII, 1785-93). This cluster calls attention to the importance of the Sea Voyage in the tale and also to the theme of healthy relationships between men and women. In addition, the words themselves that rhyme punningly are allusive. The "rime équivoque" of the noun "wente" [turn, way, or device] and the verb "wente," the preterite of "go," emphasizes the importance of travelling in the right direction without turning aside and, as in this case, travelling in accordance with the will of God. The rhyme of the noun "tyde" and the verb "betide" alludes to the Sea Voyage that is human life and to the role that is played therein by what seems to be Fortune but is actually Providence.

The idea of the Sea Voyage of life is connected metonymically to that of marriage and proper human relationships through "rime équivoque" that links the words "mariage," "corage," "viage," and "age." When Gower rhymes "mariage" and "corage," he emphasizes, as Chrétien de Troyes did before him, that "qui a le cuer, si eit le cors" (127: 3163) [he who has the heart should have the body] in lawful marriage. For example, Gower says, "thei divise/ The day and time of Mariage./ Wher love is lord of the corage,/ Him thenketh longe er that he spede" (VIII, 950-53).

Gower underscores the importance of this idea with a cluster that unites the theme of love and marriage with the idea of making public covenants: "Er thei wenten thanne atuo,/ With good herte and with good corage/ Of full Love and full mariage/ The king and he ben hol acorded./ And after, whanne it was recorded/ Unto the dowhter hou it stod,/ The yifte of al this worldes good/ Ne scolde have mad hir half so blythe" (VIII, 922-29). Metonymically, this cluster evokes the idea that there is a proper season in human life to love and marry because "age" rhymes with "corage" at one point and with "mariage" at another. Athenagoras falls in love with Thaise, and he does so at the appropriate time of life: "He that yit was of yong Age;/ So fell ther into his corage/ The lusti wo, the glade peine/ Of love" (VIII, 1761-64). Appolinus approves of the marriage, because he had always planned to find a husband for Thaise when she reached the proper age, arranging for her fostering as an infant until he "in covenable time of age/ Beset hire unto mariage" (VIII, 1305-6).

In the epitaph on Thaise's tomb, the ages of human life are specifically linked with the Sea Voyage that ends in death. The epitaph says, "Fourtiene yer sche was of Age,/ Whan deth hir tok to his viage" (VIII, 1539-40). Gower has added this phrase to the Latin, which says merely,

"Tharsiae virgini Apollonii filiae ob beneficia eivs ex aere conlato donvm dedervnt" (Kortekaas, 351) [They gave a gift made of molded bronze to Tharsia, the virgin daughter of Apollonius, because of his kindness]. Gower calls particular attention to the epitaph by both concluding it with a "rime équivoque" and beginning it with one: "O yee that this beholde,/ Lo, hier lith sche, the which was holde/ The faireste" (VIII, 1533-35). Finally, the idea of public covenants and proper speech are linked with a couplet rhyming on "-age," for Artestrathes sends his daughter to speak to Appolinus: "His doghter .../ .../ As it was thilke time usage,/ He bad to gon on his message" (VIII, 731-34). The association between love, marriage, age, speech, covenant, and the voyage of life and death is one of the devices that Gower uses to prepare us for Amans' movement from *amor* to *caritas* at the end of Book Eight. Because the purpose of his love is not to contract a marriage by making a public covenant but is to conduct a "derne" love affair, his earthly love should not prosper, in contrast to that of Appolinus and the daughter of Artestrathes.

In the cases in which Gower uses true "rime équivoque" in the tale of Appolinus, he does so to highlight key ideas, and he often uses the same rhyme more than once. The first occurs when Antiochus hangs the heads of his daughter's suitors on the gate of Antioch: "Ate laste long and late,/ For lacke of ansuere in the wise,/ The remenant that weren wise/ Enschuiden to make assay" (VIII, 370-73), and the rhyme of "wise" [manner] and "wise" [wise] calls attention to the folly of Appolinus when he goes to court the princess and to his wisdom because he can answer the riddle. The "rime équivoque" is repeated at the end of the tale when the citizens of Mittelene wish to comfort the grieving Appolinus: "Tho was ther spoke in many wise/ Amonges hem that weren wise,/ Now this, now that, bot ate laste/ The wisdom of the toun this caste,/ That yonge Taise were asent" (VIII, 1649-53). The repetition of the rhymes underscores the importance of wisdom in the "kinde" regulation of human affairs, especially since the rhyme has occurred at other places in the *Confessio* (see I, 2017-18, 2251-52, and 2767-68; II, 2673-74 and 3247-48; VI, 77-78; and VII, 2487-88 and 4379-80) to make similar points.

Gower repeats a "rime équivoque" of the noun "faile" and the verb "faile" in order to emphasize the importance of oaths and assertions in the tale, a major theme in the entire *Confessio*. Antiochus poses his riddle to Appolinus and asserts, "Who that can mi tale save,/ Al quyt he schal my doghter have;/ Of his ansuere and if he faile,/ He schal be ded withoute faile" (VIII, 411-14). The grim threat emphasizes the importance of speech and the understanding of the speech of others. Artestrathes' daughter reveals her love for Appolinus in a letter to her father, saying, "If I of him faile,/ I wot riht wel withoute faile/ Ye schull for me be dowhterles" (VIII, 901-3). As in the first case, the price of failure is death, but since

Artestrathes heeds her speech, she lives. The third use of the rhyme reminds us of the other two and echoes them; Cerymon tells Appolinus' wife, "Conforteth you:/ For trusteth wel withoute faile,/ Ther is nothing which schal you faile,/ That oghte of reson to be do" (VIII, 1214-17). His speech comforts her just as he has restored her to life by his practice of medicine.

The other examples of true "rime équivoque," like that of the preposition "lich" (VIII, 1075) and the noun "lich" (VIII, 1076) in the fourth cluster and that of the noun "wente" (VIII, 1785) and the verb "wente" (VIII, 1786) in the fifth, allude metonymically to subjects treated narratively. In addition, they occur elsewhere in the *Confessio* (see the rhyme of "wente" and "wente" in V, 2725-26).

The other metonymic rhymes in the tale are examples of "quasi" "rime équivoque," and, like those in the tale of Florent, they fall into several groups. Some rhyme on terminal derivational morphemes and bring together metonymically concepts which are related neither by sound nor by etymology. For example, after Appolinus learns that Thaise is alive, he "was arraied realy./ And out he cam al openly/ Wher Athenagoras he fond" (VIII, 1747-49). The rhyme of the two words ending in "-ly" links Appolinus' regality with the idea of being open and frank. In this way, Appolinus contrasts to Antiochus, who loves his daughter in an unnatural way, and to Amans, who wishes a "derne" love. The rhymes can also underscore the difference between concepts, as in the lines that say that Antiochus rapes his daughter "for likinge and concupiscence,/ Withoute insihte of conscience" (VIII, 293-94). In another example, the rhymes underscore the joy of the citizens of Pentapolim upon learning that the king's daughter has married the king of Tyre: "A worthi king schal ben oure lord:/ That thoghte ous ferst an hevinesse/ Is schape ous now to gret gladnesse" (VIII, 1016-18). In addition, there are "rimes équivoques" which rhyme on the final morphemes of words but which do not allude metonymically to important themes. For example, one couplet rhymes on the derivational morpheme "-al": "Singende he [Appolinus] harpeth forth withal,/ That as a vois celestial/ Hem thoghte it souneth in here Ere" (VIII, 779-81). Another couplet rhymes on "-tefied": "Where as Diane is seintefied;/ Thus stant this lady justefied" (VIII, 1269-70). Both of these couplets allude to the theme of holiness important both in the tale of Appolinus and in the *Confessio* as a whole, but they do not form part of a metonymic linguistic pattern in the tale. They do, however, contribute to the texture of the poem and show the importance of "rime équivoque."

As in other places in the *Confessio*, Gower often rhymes a word with a derivative thereof to underscore the importance of certain themes. He uses some of the same rhymes that he has used in other parts of the *Confessio*, but it is always striking that Gower chooses his "rimes équivoques" with great care to fit the particular context, one of the most noteworthy being the rhyme of "wedde" (I, 1587) and "wedde" (I, 1588) in the tale of Florent (see discussion above). Gower emphasizes that the five senses are the means to virtue or vice with a triple emphasis on sight, appropriate to the tale in which Antiochus' misuse of sight leads him to commit incest. The rhyme of "beholde" and "holde," which occurs in the first two lines of Thaise's epitaph (VIII, 1533-34) and is linked to the theme of proper relationships and the voyage of life by its placement in the epitaph, is repeated in the description of the funeral rites for Appolinus' wife: "The feste reali was holde:/ And thereto was he wel beholde" (VIII, 1563-64). The third "rime équivoque" about sight occurs when Appolinus arrives in Mittelene; the citizens "the hihe festes of Neptune/ .../ Sollempneliche thei besihe" (VIII, 1614-17) when his ship arrives. They greet him "whan thei this strange vessel syhe/ Come in" (VIII, 1618-19). All three couplets link the proper use of sight with virtuous practices.

In two cases, there occur what might be called "runs" of "rimes équivoques," passages in which two couplets occur in close proximity, calling attention to the importance of the passage rather than to themes in the tale. Two such rhymes occur within eight lines of each other in the passage in which Artestrathes and his wife decide that their daughter may marry Appolinus. Speaking of Artestrathes, Gower says, "For he wol have hire good assent,/ [He] hath for the queene hir moder sent" (VIII, 931-32), and speaking of the queen, he says that she "is thereto assented full./ Which is a dede wonderfull" (VIII, 937-38). The "run" and the echo of "assent"/ "sent" in "assented" emphasize that the marriage of Artestrathes and his wife provides a model for marriage in the tale and in the *Confessio* as a whole. A "run" of rhymes occurs also in the passage in which Appolinus guesses Antiochus' riddle, the first when Antiochus warns, "Be wel avised of this thing,/ Which hath thi lif in jeupartie" (VIII, 416-17). The second line rhymes with the line that states that "Appolinus for his partie/ .../ Unto the king he hath ansuerd" (VIII, 418-20). The second "rime équivoque" occurs in the next couplet, which describes the fact that Appolinus "hath rehersed on and on/ The pointz, and seide thereupon" (VIII, 421-22), and the "run" serves to call attention to the importance of the passage and the riddle whose solution Appolinus guesses.

An examination of Gower's use of "rime équivoque" in the tale of Appolinus shows his careful use thereof to underscore linguistically themes and ideas implicit in the narrative level of the tale both in Gower's version and in the Latin prose and verse versions. His practice in the tale of Appolinus is paradigmatic of his practice throughout the *Confessio*, and such rhymes function metonymically. If we grant Brewer's argument that in medieval poetry, metonymy is an appropriate poetic device, then we must grant that their presence in the *Confessio* and Gower's careful use thereof show that the poetic artistry of the poem is greater than has been generally conceded. In particular, Gower's use of "rime équivoque" in the tale of Appolinus, which some readers have found lacking in narrative interest or even showing Gower's lack of understanding of his Latin original, shows that the tale is poetically crafted to exemplify the narrative level metonymically. In addition, the tale shows Gower's awareness of and use of techniques from the native English poetic tradition, techniques that a modern reader must understand in order to gauge the tale's effectiveness as poetry.

Chapter Five

Type-Scenes and the Structure of Narrative:
The Sea Voyages in the Tale of Appolinus

Brewer argues that the metonymic principle governs more than the linguistic level of many medieval works, which are retellings of traditional tales in which "traditional topics and adornments may be inserted by association ..., [and] language is often formulaic, self-referring" ("Towards a Poetic" 64). He suggests that a true appreciation of Chaucer's poetry involves an understanding of his metonymic use of "traditional and popular modes that he partly inherited and partly imitated" ("Towards a Poetic" 79). Like Chaucer, Gower is an immensely learned poet who translates tales from many literary sources, and he invents a poetic idiom to recount those tales. He is important in the history of the English language because he introduces many French words (see Burch, 209, and Mossé, 314). Macaulay notes that Gower combines English and French linguistic elements and makes "a consistent and ... successful attempt to combine the French syllabic with the English accentual system of metre, ... without sacrificing the purity of the language as regards forms of words and grammatical inflexion" (Gower, vol. I: xix). As a result, many critics view Gower as a poet who writes only in the French tradition and is unaware of the native English poetic tradition. Eric W. Stockton, in contrast, observes that Gower and Chaucer "demonstrate at least some acquaintance ... with the alliterative English poetry of their day" (43). One would therefore expect Gower's poetry to have been influenced in part by the oral-formulaic tradition, which has been shown to have influenced Middle English alliterative poetry.

Some of Gower's most striking diction like "coise" is of French derivation (see Shaw, "Etymology"). In a study of Gower's vocabulary, however, Theodore H. Kaplan determines that he uses a vocabulary that is 54.9% of native English origin and only 37.9% of French origin. These percentages contrast to modern English, in which the words most often used in composition are 30.2% of native English origin and 32.7% of French origin (see 398). He speculates that if one does not study the use of "different words only" (399) as he does, "in any book of the *Confessio Amantis* the proportion of the total words of unquestioned Anglicity is the same as that for 'Langland' and Chaucer, i.e., 88 to 90 per cent" (399).

The Englishness of the *Confessio* is confirmed by the study of Ito, who shows that Gower adapts a typically French poetic device, the use of "rime équivoque," to English, with the result that the "rimes équivoques" most often used in the *Confessio* "are mostly of OE: OE type" (*John Gower* 218). Leslie F. Casson suggests that Gower uses diction which captures "the spirit of the Old English poets, and those of the alliterative revival" (188), using a mixture of French and English vocabulary as the alliterative poets do. Casson points out that Gower uses "conventional" (190) alliterative phrases (phrases which scholars now call formulaic) and words like "drake" [dragon] and "welkin" [sky], "which might have been taken straight over from an Old English poem" (188). Paul Höfer has provided a comprehensive study of Gower's use of alliterative "Formeln" (11). In addition, Gower's use of the pun on "beste" [best] and "beste" [beast] recalls the use of a similar pun on "dēor(e)," meaning either "beloved" or "beast," in *Beowulf*,[1] suggesting his affinity with the way Old English poets used puns.

In *Chaucer's Native Heritage*, Alexander Weiss analyzes the way in which Chaucer's "uniquely English quality derives from the native poetic tradition" (13). He examines the lyrics, which "may have survived as part of oral tradition" (14) and therefore may have preserved elements found in Old English poetry. Gower's use of the English tradition, as Weiss suggests of Chaucer's, is deeper than diction alone. His poetry includes, as Renoir says of other works undoubtedly composed in writing, a number of "elements clearly typical of oral-formulaic composition" ("Oral Theme" 338). Gower uses themes and type-scenes, devices that often survive in written texts long after their purpose in orally composed ones no longer exists, and he does so for reasons of literary artistry.[2]

The use of oral elements ultimately derived from Old English poetry does not imply that Gower or Chaucer knew the Old English poems that we know. Instead, it implies that they were aware of poems which used techniques like those in the extant Old English poetry. When we wish to examine themes and type-scenes, therefore, it is appropriate to study the use thereof in Old English poetry because it seems likely that the same elements were current in now-lost oral Middle English poetry and that extant Middle English poems "reflect ... characteristics common to the whole poetic corpus of the period" (Reiss, *Art* 14), oral and written. John Miles Foley has argued that "echoes from one occurrence of a given theme reverberate not simply through the ... length of the given poem, but through the collective mythic knowledge of the given culture" ("Formula and Theme" 231). Assuming, therefore, that the "collective mythic knowledge" of Middle English society contained elements of that of Old English society, I will compare Gower's work to extant Old English poems in order to illuminate the former.

The methodology most useful for an understanding of the structural levels of orally composed and oral-derived poems was outlined by Milman Parry. He provided a new way to view the Homeric poems, asserting that their style "was not a matter of individual creation, but a popular tradition, evolved by centuries of poets and audiences, which the composer of heroic verse might follow without thought of plagiarism, indeed, without knowledge that such a thing existed" (421). "Parry's great achievement," Foley argues, "lay in the fact that he was able to ... posit an ongoing traditional *process* instead of either a series of nonintegrated stages involving a *mélange* of poets, editors, and interpolators or an individual act of poetic creation" ("Oral Theory" 30) [italics Foley's]. Scholars have applied Parry's insightful ideas about the oral-formulaic tradition to texts composed in many societies. Renoir has pointed out that one "fringe benefit" ("Oral Theme" 338) of this methodology is that it enables us to understand written works which share characteristics with orally composed ones and to explain aspects of those works incomprehensible to those who seek precise written sources for all literary devices. In a recent study, Ward Parks has surveyed the scholarship devoted to Middle English poems "composed in writing yet indebted to oral traditions that underlie and inform them on many levels" (636) and shows that scholars need to understand the use of oral elements by literate poets to do justice to some poems composed in writing. I would argue that such an understanding will deepen critical perceptions of Gower.

Those scholars who have studied the presence of oral-formulaic elements in written texts have performed a great service to modern readers, especially when they have shown that the artistry of texts regarded with disfavor by twentieth-century readers is greater than normally believed because literate authors writing for literate audiences used elements of the oral-formulaic tradition. In a brief study of the *Life of Saint Alban and Saint Amphibal*, Renoir shows that John Lydgate uses the theme of the Beasts of Battle, which is not in his source. He points out that Lydgate changes the theme so that "the eagle and the wolf are ... metamorphosed from harbingers of death into protectors of the faithful and near-attestations of eternal life. For Christian readers acquainted with either the theme or the actual habits of the beasts of battle, the paradox emphasizes the immensity of God's power" ("Beasts of Battle" 457). He maintains that "the juxtaposition of the Anglo-Saxon and Lydgatian versions illustrates the kinds of change which we may expect to find in oral-formulaic themes when they occur in the written works of authors trained in a later or different tradition" ("Beasts of Battle" 457). Although Renoir acknowledges that Lydgate may have used the theme "unwittingly and possibly by sheer coincidence" ("Beasts of Battle" 457), I believe that his study demonstrates that Lydgate uses the theme purposefully. Such use shows that Lydgate is a literary artist aware of the native English poetic tradition and using elements thereof with consciousness of their literary effect. Gower makes similar use of the native English poetic tradition.

Readers of the *Confessio* often admire Gower's descriptions of the sea and of storms, especially those in the tale of Appolinus of Tyre in Book Eight. Even Macaulay, who considers it to be "almost the only story in which the interest really flags" (Gower, vol. I: xii), admires them. He even argues that "Gower's descriptions of storms at sea are especially vivid and true, so that we are led to suppose that he had had more than a mere literary acquaintance with such things" (Gower, vol. I: xiv). Ito, in contrast, suggests that because storms are conventional settings in classical literature, it is probable that Gower merely follows the Latin *Apollonius*, whose author copies his descriptions of the shipwreck of Apollonius from the *Aeneid* (see *John Gower* 67). Ito points out that the Old English translator of the *Apollonius* depicts the sea in terms of Old English conventions as well as in terms of the classical depiction of storms that he found in his Latin source. He does not, however, consider the possibility that Gower also uses a dual tradition, partly classical and partly native English.

In addition to depicting storms, the Apollonius story focuses on sea voyages, but it has not been noted that Gower's descriptions demonstrate neither realism nor the simple translation of a Latin source, but the use of the English poetic type-scene of the Sea Voyage[3] derived ultimately from Old English oral tradition. Lee C. Ramsey, who identified the type-scene, argues that such features are part of "the rhetorical tradition" (53) of Old English poetry; I believe that the type-scene was part of the English rhetorical tradition available to Gower. This tradition is found especially in alliterative Middle English poems (see Wittig, 103-34). Although the use of such devices is more frequent in alliterative than in non-alliterative works (see Stokes, "Embarcation" 12), they are also to be found in non-alliterative works like those of Lydgate. Critics who are unaware of Gower's use of the type-scene tend to make erroneous judgments about his literary artistry. For example, Lewis criticizes Gower because "when Apollonius embarks to take vengeance on the land of Tharse, the pageantry of the embarcation ... is passed over with the bald statement that the king took 'a strong pouer'" (206). In contrast, I would argue that the spareness is derived from that of the English poetic tradition, whose oral-formulaic elements leave no room for the "pageantry" of other traditions.[4]

Gower's use of the type-scene in the *Confessio* is noteworthy because he does not use it in his depiction of a sea voyage in the *Vox Clamantis*. Given how commonplace sea voyages are in European literature, we might expect Gower to depict all voyages in the same manner, regardless of his language of composition or the genre of work he is writing. Instead, he is influenced by the rhetorical tradition of the language in which he is writing, in the English *Confessio* by an oral-formulaic type-scene and in the Latin *Vox* by authors writing in Latin. As a result, the sea voyage in the *Vox* "is singularly unrealistic and heavily dependent upon lines from Ovid and ideas from Virgil" (Stockton, 6). Stockton argues that Gower uses the voyage in the *Vox* to represent the common motif of "an escape via 'The

Ship of Religion'" (366). In addition, Macaulay has pointed out that the description is heavily dependent on scenes from Ovid's *Metamorphoses*, "many hexameters being appropriated without material change" (Gower, *Vox* 379). For the convenience of the reader, Stockton prints a list of passages that Gower borrowed (see 367).

It is clear that Gower's purpose in the *Vox* is to depict the "nauem" (I, 1599) [ship] and the voyage "maris in medio" (I, 1607) [in the middle of the sea] as allegories referring to contemporary events because the prose introduction to the chapter speaks of "turrim Londoniarum" (Gower, *Vox* 66) [the Tower of London] and says, "Figurat enim dictam turrim similem esse naui prope voraginem Cille periclitanti" (Gower, *Vox* 66) [He {the narrator} indeed depicts the aforesaid tower to be like a ship near the whirlpool of Scylla the perilous]. Likewise, his references to the tempest--the "furiens pelagi ... ira" (I, 1646) [furious wrath of the sea], the "desuper emissi ... venti" (I, 1671) [winds sent from above], and the "picea ... caligine" (I, 1623) [pitch-black darkness]--are allegorical references to the Peasant's Revolt rather than references to the tempests people endure on the Sea Voyage of life as are the tempests in the tale of Appolinus in the *Confessio*. In the *Confessio*, in contrast to the *Vox*, Gower's purpose is to depict sea voyages in terms of the native English formulaic tradition, and he evokes thereby the images traditionally evoked by the type-scene. In order to discuss Gower's use of the type-scene, one must understand its use in Old English poetry. It is helpful to compare Gower's use to that of the *Beowulf* poet because the clearest surviving examples of the type-scene are in *Beowulf*.

Ramsey states that the two sea voyages in *Beowulf* are similar "in events and in the sequence of events" (54) and that they illustrate "general correspondence without actual repetition" (56). Ramsey analyzes the paradigmatic structure of the type-scene in *Beowulf* as follows: "Beowulf gives an order to his men ... and explains the purpose of his voyage. ... He leads the way to the ship ... which waits at the shore laden with treasures. ... The men depart in the ship and sail until they can observe the opposite shore. ... They moor the ship ... and are greeted by a coastal guardian. ... They leave the ship and proceed to the hall" (55). He notes that even a poet composing in a completely oral tradition treats "his conventional themes at greater or lesser length depending on his specific intent" (57). In addition, the particular names which Ramsey assigns to elements--especially the "treasure" with which the ship is laden, the "coastal guardian," and the "royal hall"--are specific to the situation in *Beowulf*. A general pattern underlies the type-scene as identified by Ramsey: the ship is laden with some form of valuable cargo, the hero is greeted by someone on the shore, and he visits the domicile of a king or other important person.

Understanding the paradigmatic pattern that lies behind the Sea Voyage resembles that of understanding the theme known as the Hero on the Beach. In the poems studied by David K. Crowne, the hero is on a literal beach, and it was not until Renoir pointed out that the "beach" is one variant of a more general pattern in which the hero "stands at the juncture between ... two worlds" ("Oral-Formulaic Theme Survival" 73) that scholars truly began to understand the use of the theme. The terms identified by Ramsey likewise represent a broader range of possibilities than that implied by the terms themselves. Gower treats the Sea Voyage with great freedom, but the paradigm underlies his passages.

One important question that the critic must consider is whether Gower and his audience could have been familiar with the type-scene of the Sea Voyage and therefore reacted to it rather than merely perceiving the voyages as rhetorically embellished passages. The fact that Gower uses the type-scene in places other than the tale of Appolinus and that he uses all the elements of it at various times indicates that we are justified in assuming that his use was deliberate and that he expected his audience to appreciate it. In many places, his use derives power from the fact that the type-scene provides an antithesis to what the audience might logically expect. In Book Three, for example, the Greeks "tornen hom ayein" (III, 977) from Troy, and they sail until beset by a tempest. Because of the storm, King Namplus lights fires designed to wreck the Greek fleet by bringing it onto the rocks, and "this Flete, which an havene soghte,/ The bryghte fyres sih a ferr" (III, 1038-39). The Greeks have embarked, their ships loaded, as Gower and his audience know, with treasure plundered from Troy, and they sail until they see the fires on the shore of Namplus' country. Instead of anchoring the ships, being greeted by a coastal guardian, and going to the palace, the Greeks drown when their ships drive "al to pieces on the roche" (III, 1048), or they are forced to retreat. Namplus' inhospitality is underscored when we remember the hospitality that normally greets a hero after his voyage.

One of the places where Gower uses all of the elements of the type-scene is in his description of Appolinus' fourth voyage; it matches the paradigmatic type-scene closely. Appolinus decides to leave Pentapolim, and we know that his destination, "Tyr" (VIII, 1010), has been revealed because "every man it hadde in speche" (VIII, 1014). After "Appolinus his leve tok" (VIII, 1021), "to schip he goth" (VIII, 1029) and embarks. The ship is full of treasure, and Appolinus puts "of gold ... Sommes grete" (VIII, 1119) in his wife's coffin. After the burial of his seemingly dead wife, Appolinus "seileth, til that he may winne/ The havene of Tharse" (VIII, 1274-75). When he has "aryved ther" (VIII, 1276), he is greeted by "al the toun at ones" (VIII, 1279). After he disembarks, he goes "to his In" (VIII, 1285), leaving the valuable "cargo" of the ship, his "doghter Thaise" (VIII, 1295), in the city. The last episode parallels the concluding element of the second use of the type-scene in *Beowulf*, in which Beowulf gives the treasure given him by Hrothgar to Hygelac, leading us to speculate that one paradigmatic ending of the type-scene involved the distribution of treasure.

Gower departs from his Latin sources in order to depict the voyage in terms of the Old English type-scene. In Gotfried's *Pantheon*, the scene is so brief that the sea voyage is hardly mentioned. Gotfried places his emphasis on the dialogue between Apollonius and Archistrates. The rejoicing Apollonius tells Archistrates that "mortuus Antiochus rex est" (159: 195) [King Antiochus has died]. Archistrates makes the arrangements for the journey, telling Apollonius to take "gemmas, aurum" (160: 220) [gems and gold] and his "sponsa[m]" (160: 222) [wife] and to depart to "suscipe[re] regna" (160: 225) [take up his royal powers]. Apollonius then "pergit" (160: 226) [proceeds] on the sea, where his wife gives birth during a tempest.

Even the author of the Latin prose version puts little emphasis on the voyage itself.[5] Indeed, Gower has changed the scene substantially, for in the Latin prose,[6] King Archistrates, not Apollonius, gives the orders that initiate the voyage. "Gaudio" (Kortekaas, 327) [With joy], Apollonius tells the news "ad patrem" (Kortekaas, 327) [to her father]. As in Gotfried's *Pantheon*, Archistrates makes the arrangements for the voyage. Although the orders are not necessarily given by the person making the sea voyage (in the Old English *Elene*, it is Constantine, not Elene, who gives the order that initiates the voyage), it is usually the voyager who gives the order. Gower's change makes the episode fit the paradigm more closely than the Latin version does. Archistrates orders his daughter to be accompanied by "nutricem suam Lycoridem et obstetricem peritissimam" (Kortekaas, 329) [her nurse Lycorides and an extremely experienced midwife] because he knows that she will be giving birth during the sea voyage. Although Apollonius is seen "ascendentes nauem cum multa familia multoque apparatu" (Kortekaas, 329) [boarding the ship with a large household and with great splendor] and, according to the version in recension RA, "copia" (Kortekaas, 328) [with troops], enough elements reminiscent of the type-scene are not present in the Latin to say that Gower merely translated his source accurately.

When not all of the elements of the type-scene are present in a particular episode of Gower's tale of Appolinus, those that are present occur in the precise order noted by Ramsey. Especially in the hands of a literate author, the elements of oral-formulaic themes and type-scenes function in a way similar to that in which the "component parts" (Propp, 19) of the European folk-tale function. Vladimir Propp argues that "the functions of the dramatis personae are basic components of the tale" (21), that "the number of functions ... is limited" (21) [italics deleted], and that "the sequence of functions is always identical" (22) [italics deleted]. He shows that not all tales "give evidence of all functions" (22), although "the absence of certain functions does not change the order of the rest" (22). Gower is noted for his "narrative directness and tautness" (Wickert, 215), and he omits elements extraneous to a particular voyage. The omission of some elements, however, does not affect the order of those that he uses. In the tale of Appolinus, the fifth and sixth voyages of Appolinus are described with great brevity, and the seventh voyage begins without the elements that normally initiate the type-scene. In all three cases, all the elements that are present occur in the proper order.

As Appolinus' fifth voyage begins, "he takth his leve and torneth/ To Schipe, and goth him hom to Tyr" (VIII, 1310-11), and we see his arrival from the point of view of the coast-guards, who see "the Schip com in seilinge" (VIII, 1314). Disembarking, Appolinus is greeted by "every man" (VIII, 1312) of the city instead of by a single person. Appolinus' sixth voyage begins when he "besoghte/ Suche of his lordes as he wolde,/ That thei with him to Tharse scholde,/ To fette his doghter Taise there" (VIII, 1568-71). This statement gives both his destination and his order to depart. "Thei anon al redy were" (VIII, 1572), and he leads them "to schip" (VIII, 1573). They sail "til thei the havene of Tharse hente" (VIII, 1574), where "they londe" (VIII, 1575), are greeted, and are led, not to a hall, but to the "tombe" (VIII, 1581) of Thaise.

Appolinus' seventh voyage begins without the elements of the type-scene that normally initiate a Sea Voyage, presumably because the voyage follows so closely on the sixth that such details would be unnecessarily repetitious. Appolinus leaves Tharse, "seilende toward Tyr ayein" (VIII, 1591). As a result of a tempest, the mariners do not reach Tyre, but "tofor the wynd thei dryve,/ Til longe and late thei aryve/ With gret distresce, as it was sene,/ Upon this toun of Mitelene" (VIII, 1607-10). After the ship "hath his Seil avaled" (VIII, 1619) and has been moored, the Tyrians are greeted by "the lordes bothe and the comune" (VIII, 1613), who are performing the rites of Neptune "upon the stronde at the rivage" (VIII, 1615). Appolinus does not leave the ship and go to the palace; instead, in an inversion of the expected element, "the lord which of the cite was,/ Whos name is Athenagoras" (VIII, 1621-22), comes to visit him as he lies in the darkness.

In these three incidents in the Latin prose, the elements of the type-scene are not present. The sixth voyage of Apollonius is not described at all: the author says merely, "Apollonius uenit Tharso $IIII^{to.}$ decimo transacto" (Kortekaas, 363) [Apollonious came to Tharse after fourteen years had passed]. The fifth voyage occupies a portion of a single sentence: "Nauem ascendit: ignotas et longas petiit Aegypti regiones" (Kortekaas, 339) [He boarded a ship: he reached the unknown and distant regions of Egypt]. His seventh voyage begins when "nauigat ... Tiro reuersurus" (Kortekaas, 367) [he sails in order to return to Tyre]; according to RA, "altum pelagum petiit" (Kortekaas, 366) [he headed for the deep sea]. Gower has changed the scene of the arrival in Mitelene in order to evoke the type-scene. In the prose, the people of Mitelene are celebrating "Neptunalia" (Kortekaas, 367) [religious rites in honor of Neptune], but the scene emphasizes the grief of Apollonius. When he arrives, he "ingemuit" (Kortekaas, 367) [sighed], uttering a lament because others rejoice while he grieves. Although Athenagoras visits the ship, in the context of the Latin prose, his visit does not recall the expected end of the type-scene.

Inversions analogous to that in the tale of Namplus are often found in the tale of Appolinus, a fact which suggests that Gower deliberately plays with the expectations his audience would have had about the Sea Voyage. The second and third voyages of Appolinus show that Gower sometimes depicts sea voyages in a way that varies from that found in Old English poetry, and from these scenes, a reader can understand that an author trained in a literate poetic tradition changes the type-scene for literary reasons.

Instead of giving an order and explaining the purpose of his second voyage, Appolinus, who wishes to "forsake ... his oghne lond" (VIII, 460) in order to escape the enmity of Antiochus, "withoute take leve,/ Als priveliche as evere he myhte,/ ... goth him to the See be nyhte" (VIII, 466-68). He embarks "in Schipes that be whete laden" (VIII, 469), and the wheat is the precious cargo that represents treasure. The seamen "hale up Seil and forth thei fare" (VIII, 471), and Appolinus sails until he sees his destination: "He hath his rihte cours forth holde/ Be Ston and nedle, til he cam/ To Tharse, and there his lond he nam" (VIII, 540-42). Although he is not greeted by a coastal guardian, he leaves the ship and takes "herbergage" (VIII, 548) with "a Burgeis riche of gold and fee" (VIII, 543), the middle-class equivalent of the royal hall. Because of the famine in the city, Appolinus gives "al freliche of his oghne yifte/ His whete" (VIII, 555-56), as he leaves Thaise in Tharse at the end of his fourth voyage and Beowulf gives gifts to Hygelac when he has returned to Geatland. Appolinus is more generous than Apollonius in Gotfried's *Pantheon*, who sells much of his grain: "Copia frumenti populo prestatur ementi,/ atque dedit gratis pondera multa satis" (154: 35) [Abundance of grain is offered to the people who wish to buy, and he gave quite great weights for nothing]. The change seems motivated by Gower's desire to depict Appolinus as a treasure-giver.

Appolinus' third voyage also begins without an explanation of the purpose thereof, because Appolinus wishes to hide both his purpose and his destination, but the statement "And thoghte he wolde his place change/ And seche a contre more strange" (VIII, 595-96) reminds us of the element that normally occurs. After taking leave of the "Tharsiens" (VIII, 597), Appolinus "is to Schipe gon" (VIII, 598), although since the wheat has been distributed, the ship is not laden with treasure. The "Schipmen" (VIII, 608) are unable to moor the ship, for "er thei to londe myhte aproche,/ The

Schip toclef upon a roche,/ And al goth doun into the depe" (VIII, 625-27). Appolinus reaches the coast "one" (VIII, 634) and is greeted by a benevolent "Fisshere" (VIII, 646), who plays the role of the coastal guardian. After that, Appolinus goes to the Middle English equivalent of the hall, to "Pentapolim,/ Wher bothe king and queene duellen" (VIII, 658-59).

In both cases, Gower has departed from his Latin source in order to depict the voyages in terms of the English type-scene, a departure not found in the Old English prose, which translates the Latin with greater fidelity in this respect than does Gower. The Latin and Old English authors scarcely mention the two voyages, emphasizing in the first case the distribution of wheat and in the second the shipwreck Apollonius endures. When Antiochus orders "classes nauium preparare" (Kortekaas, 289) [fleets of ships to be prepared] to pursue Apollonius--"scipa gegéarcian and him æfter faran" (Goolden, *Old English "Apollonius"* 10) [them to prepare ships and travel after him] according to the Old English prose--he learns that Apollonius has already fled. Before Antiochus' ships can be made ready, "ueniens Apollonius Tarsum euasit" (Kortekaas, 291) [Apollonius, coming to Tharse, escaped]--he "becom ... to Tharsum" (Goolden, *Old English "Apollonius"* 10) [came to Tharse], according to the Old English prose. Although Apollonius is greeted upon his arrival by Hellanicus and proceeds to the city, the scene places little emphasis on the voyage because it combines it with Antiochus' attempt to pursue the fleeing Apollonius. When Apollonius leaves Tharse for Pentapolim, the Latin says merely that "qui dum ... nauigat" (Kortekaas, 297) [while he sails], a tempest arises and the ship is wrecked; the Old English says, "Hig ongunnon þa rowan" (Goolden, *Old English "Apollonius"* 16) [Then they began to sail] before describing the tempest that brings it about that "þæt scip eal tobærst" (Goolden, *Old English "Apollonius"* 16) [all that ship burst apart]. Gower uses the type-scene, albeit in a way that differs from the paradigm found in Old English poetry.

Edward B. Irving, Jr., argues that the purpose of the Sea Voyages in *Beowulf* is to "characterize the hero by dramatizing his habitual mode of action" (49), and Ramsey comments that "the crossing of the sea is an ordinary but characteristic challenge" (57) to Beowulf, a situation also found in the voyages in the legend of Apollonius of Tyre. Gower uses the type-scene of the Sea Voyage to characterize the hero, Appolinus, and his heroic daughter, Thaise, as well as, by inversion of the usual pattern, the villainous Taliart.

The voyage of Thaise presents an unusual form of the type-scene, because she is a maiden, not a hero. Instead of giving an order, she calls out, "Ha mercy, help for goddes sake" (VIII, 1395). The thieves hear her, and "into the barge thei hire take,/ As thieves scholde, and forth thei wente" (VIII, 1396-97). Thaise herself is the valuable cargo with which the ship is laden, because after arriving in Mitelene, the shipmaster "profreth Thaise forto selle" (VIII, 1409). The thieves sail "til ate laste thei aryve/ At Mitelene the Cite" (VIII, 1404-5), anchor there, and are greeted by "Leonin ...,/ Which Maister of the bordel was" (VIII, 1410-11). Thaise is then led, not to a palace, but to a "bordel" (VIII, 1423), where she acts in a heroic but womanly fashion to protect her integrity. In the Latin prose, in contrast, Tharsia does not call for help (a maidenly action analogous to a hero giving orders). Instead, while she is praying, "subito pirate apparuerunt" (Kortekaas, 347) [pirates suddenly appeared], and they simply "alto pelago petierunt" (Kortekaas, 347) [made for the deep sea]. In Gower's tale, the fact that they take her into the ship inverts the normal pattern of the type-scene, in which the hero leads his men to the ship. Furthermore, instead of being greeted by Leonin--a named character who is the inversion of the coastal guardian--the pirates in the Latin prose put Tharsia on sale "inter cetera mancipia" (Kortekaas, 351) [among other slaves], and a nameless "leno" (Kortekaas, 353) [procurer] buys her. By using the type-scene, Gower emphasizes that a woman may be called on to play the hero's role when she lacks male protectors. This fact heightens the passivity of Antiochus' daughter as she participates in her father's sin and the justness of the fact that she shares his punishment.

In the Latin legend, only the voyage of Taliart is depicted in terms that are reminiscent of the Old English type-scene. Taliart's voyage begins, not with his orders, but with those of the "rex" (Kortekaas, 285) [king], recalling the fact that the type-scene in *Elene* begins with the command given by Constantine. In contrast to Constantine, whose purpose is benevolent, and presumably to other kings, Antiochus "uocauit ... dispensatorem suum" (Kortekaas, 285) [called his steward], ordering him to kill Apollonius. The Old English translator says that Antiochus "gecigde his dihtnere" (Goolden, *Old English "Apollonius"* 8) [called his steward], ordering that he "acwel[eþ]" (Goolden, *Old English "Apollonius"* 8) [kill] Apollonius. The Latin Taliart, "assumens pecuniam" (Kortekaas, 287) [taking money] and, according to recension RA, "uenenum" (Kortekaas, 286) [poison], "petiit patriam innocentis" (Kortekaas, 287) [sought the country of the innocent man]; the Old English Taliart, "genám mid him ge feoh ge attor and on scip astah and for æfter þam unscæddian Apollonie oð ðæt he to his eðle becom" (Goolden, *Old English "Apollonius"* 8) [took with him both money and poison and went on a ship and travelled after the innocent Apollonius until he came to his {Apollonius'} native land]. The Latin Taliart "superuenit" (Kortekaas, 289) [arrived] in Tyre ("becom" [came], according to the Old English [Goolden, *Old English "Apollonius"* 8]). After learning that Apollonius has departed, he returns to Antioch. In the Latin and Old English versions of the legend, Antiochus gives an order and explains the purpose of the journey, and Taliart embarks on the ship, taking with him treasure. He sails until he reaches Tyre; then he disembarks secretly and goes to the city.

Gower translates the passage accurately, but he places more emphasis on the journey itself than do the Latin and Old English texts, with the result that the type-scene appears clearly. As in the Latin and Old English, Gower's Antiochus, speaking to Taliart, "bad him go/ Strawht unto Tyr" (VIII, 508-9), explaining that the purpose of the journey is to kill "the Prince" (VIII, 511). After receiving his orders, Taliart "in a Galeie/ With alle haste he tok his weie" (VIII, 513-14), and "he saileth blyve,/ Til he tok lond upon the ryve/ Of Tyr" (VIII, 515-17). Because his journey is surreptitious, he is greeted by no coastal guardian, and "al anon/ Into the Burgh he gan to gon" (VIII, 517-18). When he learns that Appolinus has left Tyre, he returns to Antioch, but his journey is not described. I should like to suggest that Gower, reading the Latin description of Taliart's journey, was reminded of the type-scene of his native poetic tradition.

In Old English poetry, the Sea Voyage type-scene is used to depict heroic figures, whereas Taliart is a villain,[7] and one can assume that the type-scene known to Gower and his audience also depicted heroes. Gower changed the voyages made by Appolinus, Taliart, and Thaise to depict them all in terms of the type-scene, using the inversions in the voyages of Taliart and Thaise to emphasize the fact that Appolinus is a true hero and, at the end of the poem, a great king, just as Beowulf is after his voyages. When Taliart's journey occurs in a context that includes many uses of the type-scene, it recalls the others, and Taliart's villainy is made clear by negative inversion: he does not give orders, but follows evil ones; he takes poison as well as treasure on his voyage; he is not greeted by welcoming people; and his return voyage is not described, whereas all the voyages of Appolinus are depicted in terms of the type-scene.

From Appolinus' first sea voyage to his last one, Gower uses the type-scene. The Latin prose describes Apollonius' first voyage simply: "Nauigans adtingit Antiocham" (Kortekaas, 283) [Voyaging, he reached Antioch], rendered by the Old English prose translator as "Agan rowan od þæt he becom to Antiochian" (Goolden, *Old English "Apollonius"* 6) [He began to sail until he came to Antioch]. In Gower's tale of Appolinus, the first voyage presents a brief version of the type-scene, and Gower explains the purpose when Appolinus lies "musende on a nyht" (VIII, 380) about Antiochus' daughter, so that "he thoghte assaie hou that it ferde" (VIII, 382). Although we do not hear him give the order to depart, Gower tells us that "he was with worthi compainie/ Arraied, and with good navie/ To schipe he goth" (VIII, 383-85). After the embarcation, "the wynd him dryveth,/ And seileth, til that he arryveth" (VIII, 385-86), and after the ship is "sauf in the port of Antioche/ He londeth, and goth to aproche/ The kinges Court and his presence" (VIII, 387-89). In the interests of succinct narration, Gower presumably chose not to include elements extraneous to this voyage, the treasures in the ship, the observation of the shore, and the greeting given by the coastal guardian. Nevertheless, just as Beowulf's first sea voyage culminates with his fight against the humanoid monster Grendel who eats human beings, that of Appolinus culminates in his encounter with the monster in human form Antiochus and the riddle about the speaker who says, "I ete .../ Mi modres fleissh" (VIII, 406-7). The similarity suggests that the type-scene often depicted the hero as one who conquered monsters.

As the narrative draws to a close, Gower uses the type-scene to emphasize the regality of Appolinus and his command over others, an emphasis found in neither the Latin nor the Old English versions. Before leaving Mitelene on his eighth voyage, Appolinus recounts the treachery of Strangulio and Dionise to Athenagoras. He next "seide hou in his compaignie/ His doghter and himselven eke/ Schull go vengance forto seke" (VIII, 1780-82). In the Latin, he was simply "cum eo [Athenagoras] et cum filia uolens per Tharsum" (Kortekaas, 399) [inclined to go to Tyre with him {Athenagoras} and his daughter]. They do not sail to Tharse, because Appolinus has a vision in which he is told "to seile into an other stede" (VIII, 1792), Ephesus. When the wind changes in the morning, Appolinus gives a new order: He "bad the Maister make him yare,/ Tofor the wynd for he wol fare/ To Ephesim" (VIII, 1811-13).

In the Latin prose, Appolinus "iussit" (Kortekaas, 399) [ordered] his "gubernatori" (Kortekaas, 399) [helmsman] to sail to Ephesus, but he does so on the advice of Tharsia and Athenagoras, a fact which makes his regality less than it is in Gower's tale. After his vision, Apollonius "indicat genero et filie, somnium, et illi dixerunt: 'Fac, domine, quod tibi uidetur'" (Kortekaas, 399) [makes known his dream to his son-in-law and daughter, and they said, "Sir, do what seems good to you"]. In Gower's version, the episode clearly presents the type-scene. Appolinus sails until coming "unto the stede/ Where as he scholde londe" (VIII, 1814-15), whereupon "he londeth" (VIII, 1815). In the Latin prose, he orders the helmsman "Ephesum petere" (Kortekaas, 399) [to go to Ephesus]; upon arrival, he visits the temple after "descendens" (Kortekaas, 399) [disembarking]. In Gower's tale of Appolinus, Appolinus disembarks formally in the morning, and with Thaise, Athenagoras, and "a gret route in compaignie" (VIII, 1825), he goes to "the temple" (VIII, 1824) where he is reunited with his wife. His journey to the temple takes the place of that to the hall.

Appolinus leaves Ephesus on his ninth voyage, and he gives orders, for "he seith he wol holde his cours to Tyr" (VIII, 1888). In the Latin and Old English versions, in contrast, he gives no orders but "nauem ascendit" (Kortekaas, 405) [boarded the ship], and "for ða siddan to Tirum" (Goolden, *Old English "Apollonius"* 38) [travelled then to Tyre] according to the Old English prose. In the Latin prose, while in Tyre, he makes Athenagoras king and immediately leaves for Tharse, without giving orders. The text gives one almost no indication that a new voyage is beginning: "Et constituit regem loco suo Athenagoram generum suum. Et cum eo et cum filia sua et cum exercitu nauigans uenit Tharsum" (Kortekaas, 405) [He appointed Athenagoras his son-in-law king in his country, and with him, his daughter, and an army, he came sailing to Tharse]. In the Old English prose, he "gesette" (Goolden, *Old English "Apollonius"* 38) [appointed] Athenagoras "to cynge" (Goolden, *Old English "Apollonius"* 38) [as king]. Finally, "for ða soðlice þanon to Tharsum" (Goolden, *Old English "Apollonius"* 38) [he then truly went thence to Tharse]. In Gower's tale, the embarkation is not described, but the other elements of the type-scene are present: "Forth they go,/ And striken nevere, til thei come/ To Tyr, where as thei havene nome,/ And londen hem" (VIII, 1890-93). They are greeted by many people and travel to the palace, where "the king hath take his real place,/ The queene is into chambre go" (VIII, 1902-3). As a result, the passage ends in a way appropriate to the type-scene.

In Gower's tale of Appolinus, Appolinus begins his tenth voyage by giving an order: He "seide thanne he wolde wende/ To Tharse, forto make an ende/ Of that his doghter was betraied" (VIII, 1921-23). He takes "strong pouer with him" (VIII, 1927) and embarks. The mariners "seilen, til thei come alonde/ At Tharse nyh to the cite" (VIII, 1932-33); the citizens of the town greet Appolinus and "don him reverence" (VIII, 1935). Appolinus and the Tharsians do not go to a hall but go to a law court, where they condemn "the tretour Strangulio/ And Dionise" (VIII, 1937-38). In Gotfried's *Pantheon*, the emphasis is on the trial, and in the Latin and Old English prose versions, it is on the trial and on Thaise's generosity to Theophilus in the Latin and to Theophilus and Philothemia in the Old English. By shortening the scenes of trial and pardon, Gower places the emphasis on the sea voyage.

As Gower's Appolinus begins his eleventh and last voyage, he leaves Tharse and goes to Pentapolim, because his father-in-law has died and he has succeeded to the throne. His regality is emphasized because the citizens of Pentapolim have sent him a letter in which they "him preiden, as here liege lord,/ That he the lettre wel conceive/ And come his regne to receive" (VIII, 1972-74). "He tok his leve" (VIII, 1980) of the Tharsians, "goth him into Schipe ayein" (VIII, 1981), and sails until "thei Pentapolim have take" (VIII, 1984). Gotfried's *Pantheon* says merely that Apollonius "visitat Archistratem" (177: 592) [visits Archistrates]. In the Latin and Old English prose, Apollonius receives no letter but "nauigat cum suis ad Pentapolim" (Kortekaas, 409) [sails with his family to Pentapolim--"for siddan on scipe to Pentapolim" (Goolden, *Old English "Apollonius"* 40) [went afterwards on ship to Pentapolim], according to the Old English prose. Archistrates is still alive and is pleased to see "neptem cum matre" (Kortekaas, 409) [his granddaughter and her mother], and he gives "medietatem regni sui Appollonio

... et medietatem filie sue" (Kortekaas, 409) [half his kingdom to Apollonius and half to his daughter]. According to the Old English prose, "he becwæd healf his rice Apollonio, healf his dohtor" (Goolden, *Old English "Apollonius"* 42) [bequeathed half his kingdom to Apollonius, half to his daughter]. Both versions emphasize the generosity of Archistrates. In contrast, Gower's tale of Appolinus ends in a way that recalls the last third of *Beowulf*, in which the hero is shown to be worthy of the kingship because of his heroism, suggesting that the Sea Voyage often shows a poem's audience the nature of true kingliness.

The sea voyages contribute to Gower's depiction of Appolinus as a hero who matures into a good king, but there is a deeper meaning both to the type-scene and to the voyages in Gower's tale. Ramsey comments that in *Beowulf*, the sea "stands as a barrier separating man from man and nation from nation, a barrier with which the heroes of the poem have always to contend" (57). The sea is also a barrier for Appolinus, Thaise, and Taliart, emblematic of the barriers with which both good and evil people must contend in Book Eight of the *Confessio*, an emphasis not found in the light-hearted Latin prose romance, with its emphasis on adventure, sex, and verbal wit, nor in Gotfried's *Pantheon* and the Old English prose. The emphasis on barriers fits the dramatic device of the *Confessio Amantis*, in which Amans must learn to deal with the barriers to his love consisting of the lady's "daunger" (I, 2443) and his own "Elde" (VIII, 2828).

Ramsey argues that the sea voyage is particularly significant because it is "symbolic of the journey of death" (58). Since one of the themes of the Apollonius legend is death and rebirth--Apollonius' wife, for example, appears to die on a voyage and is reborn at the end of it--Gower presumably uses the Sea Voyage type-scene to deepen the resonances of the theme and make it obvious to his audience emotionally as well as intellectually. As the last contained narrative in the *Confessio*, the tale of Appolinus, with its emphasis on death and rebirth, is appropriate for the conclusion of the poem. Acknowledging that he is old and that he is in "the Wynter [that] wol no Somer knowe" (VIII, 2853), Amans is spiritually reborn. Amans leaves earthly *amor* for the love of God and a life of prayer, and Gower concludes the *Confessio* with a hope for the final rebirth of the members of his audience in the life of Heaven: "So that above in thilke place/ Wher resteth love and alle pes,/ Our joie mai ben endeles" (VIII, 3170-72).

Ramsey sums up the importance of the type-scene of the Sea Voyage as follows: "The sea voyages of *Beowulf* have both a symbolic and a broader structural significance: symbolically, they help link together the major themes of voyaging, battle, challenge, and death; structurally, they ... mark off the beginning and ending of the narrative as well as the transitions between its major segments" (59). As I have shown, Gower adapts the material he has borrowed from a Latin source so that the sea voyages play an important symbolic and structural role in his version of the legend, marking, as in *Beowulf*, the transitions between major episodes.

Stokes notes that one's response to a theme "will be influenced not only by what it is in itself, but by conscious or subconscious perception of the type to which it belongs; by the associations, expectations, and mood the scene will have accrued to itself and will here evoke; by the relation of the present instance of it both to other instances elsewhere ... and to the specific narrative context in question" ("Embarcation" 24). In Book Eight of the *Confessio*, the advantage Gower has by adapting a type-scene lies in the fact that such traditional elements follow the "metonymic rule of thumb" that governs "all formulaic diction": they "conjure a network of essential ideas, so that a poet and audience ...--and, to a lesser degree, the modern reader alive to traditional method--will experience the present poem against the backdrop of the poetic tradition" (Foley, "*Beowulf*" 135). The type-scene thus alludes to elements both within the tale of Appolinus and in the entire *Confessio* as well as to elements of an originally oral tradition. Because he can use techniques of versification and story-telling borrowed from continental sources and elements from the vernacular poetic tradition, Gower's poetry has a type of artistry seldom understood in the twentieth century.

Chapter Six

"Of Storial Thyng":
The Relationship of the Tales
of Gower and Chaucer Reconsidered

In this study, I have argued that attention to the linguistic nature of the *Confessio Amantis* on both large and small levels reveals that it is a work of considerable literary artistry. This fact is not surprising for a major work of literature written during the Middle Ages because medieval authors were deeply concerned with "the nature and function of language" (Vance, 293). In a study of Chaucer's *Troilus and Criseyde*, Eugene Vance discusses medieval ideas about "the relationship between the order of verbal signs and social order" and the way a poet was able to "incorporate this metalinguistic consciousness into his strategies of composition" (293-94). Two poets writing in the same country and age and recounting the same traditional tales in the same vernacular language must have been guided by the same "metalinguistic consciousness." Gower and Chaucer are remarkably similar, and both respect "tradition and authority, proverbial lore, stories from antiquity, and old books" (Dean, 402); an understanding of their shared "metalinguistic consciousness" helps us understand the poetry of both. Only if one appreciates the similarities between Gower and Chaucer can one understand the ways in which they differ, for example, the contrast between the digressions in the *Canterbury Tales* and "the brief generalizing passages" (Smallwood, 440) in the *Confessio*.

The problem with considering the "metalinguistic consciousness" of Gower and Chaucer and with dealing comparatively with their works is that, as Cooper points out, "Chaucer criticism has tended to take the form of constructing hypothesis upon hypothesis" (64), especially in the absence of facts on which to build theories. In no areas has the tendency to build hypothetical models been more apparent than in those concerning the relationship between Gower and Chaucer as men and between their works considered as literature.

Robinson observes that from Chaucer's life records as well as from references in the *Confessio* and *Troilus*, we can guess that Gower and Chaucer "were in friendly, if not intimate relations" (Chaucer, xxvii). Much more has been hypothesized; for example, Diller has speculated that Gower omitted the allusion to Chaucer from his revision of Book Eight because he had "hoped to earn favours [from Richard II] which so far had been reserved for the younger poet [Chaucer]" (51), failed, and then wrote a "revised version [which] was quickly successful with Henry of Lancaster" (51). Much speculation about the relationship between the men is related to speculation about their works, especially of the references to the tales of Canace and Appolinus in the *Man of Law's Prologue*. Some critics believe, to quote Howard as a typical example, that the *Prologue* may represent "Chaucer's amusing response to Gower's urging that he return from fabliaux to more moral matters: 'if I've told fornication, you've told incest'" (Howard, 46). A reading of Howard's study may suggest that this remark led to a breach between the two because Gower lacked a sense of humor. The problem is that such details, although often reported as facts, are not documentable from the life records of the two men.

The tendency to build hypotheses in the absence of historical knowledge and apply them to literary works has affected the criticism of medieval literature adversely. Few Middle English scholars have taken notice of the warning made by William L. Sullivan in 1953: "Because the Man of Law refers to Chaucer explicitly and to Gower implicitly, it has been taken for granted that these are Chaucer's own views" (1). An informed literary reading does not consider the Man of Law "as a mere mouthpiece of Chaucer, who takes advantage of this opportunity to give a prospectus of a work he has not yet completed and at the same time to criticize, on a delicate point, one of his most famous contemporaries, John Gower, who had recently made a complimentary reference to him" (1). Stanley B. Greenfield has pointed out that the only fruitful approach to a poem involves dealing with it on its own terms so that the scholar "work[s] from the poem itself outwards" (100) rather than applying preconceived ideas thereto. I should like to suggest that we must "work outwards" from the poems of Gower and Chaucer to determine what they themselves tell us.

Sullivan's interpretation of the *Man of Law's Prologue* is more sophisticated than those of many other critics who either preceded or followed him (for example, Alfred David, who views the Man of Law as a fictionalized portrait of Gower). It is based on an appreciative understanding of Chaucer's humor rather than on a denigration of Gower. Sullivan points out that "if Dickens had created a character with pretensions to literary knowledge who discussed Dickens's works, naming several novels that he did not write, and referring to Jane Austen as vulgar, it is doubtful that any of his contemporaries would have concluded that he had forgotten his own works or Jane Austen's. They would have concluded that he deliberately misrepresented them--for comic effect" (6). He argues that Chaucer is making just such a deliberate comic misrepresentation. Sullivan suggests that the Man of Law includes works found in the *Confessio* but not in the *Legend of Good Women* in his list of tales from the latter because the Man of Law is confusing two similar works. He also points out that Chaucer has the Man of Law include a detail from the Latin *Apollonius* which Gower did not include (see 6-7). He argues that assuming that the *Prologue* praises Chaucer and denigrates Gower is dubious because "it is a very strained sort of praise which says in effect: 'At least he does not write about incest'" (7).

Sullivan's analysis helps us recover some of the humor of the *Man of Law's Prologue* that has been missed by critics using the biographical approach. I would argue that it frees us to appreciate aspects of the humor of the *Canterbury Tales* as a whole. There are lines at the end of the unfinished *Squire's Tale* which suggest that it will involve incest: "And after wol I speke of Cambalo,/ That faught in lystes with the bretheren two/ For Canacee er that he myghte hire wynne" (Chaucer, 134: 667-69). Haldeen Braddy believes that Chaucer abandoned the *Squire's Tale* because he discovered that the romance he was translating involved incest (see 289). In contrast, I should like to suggest that if the completed *Squire's Tale* was indeed to involve incest, then Chaucer is making a sophisticated joke in the *Man of Law's Prologue*: the Man of Law grudgingly praises Chaucer for never having committed a literary crime which he intends to commit later in the *Canterbury Tales*.

If we free ourselves from the pseudo-biographies of Gower and Chaucer based on hypothesis rather than fact, we are able to turn to their works without preconceived notions about them. Fisher points out that although scholars have studied carefully most major influences on Chaucer, "the parallels between his work and Gower's have not hitherto received full consideration" (302). Such consideration is, however, beginning to be given. Cherniss observes that the *Confessio* appears "in the wake of Chaucer's experiments with the vision form and may well owe its generic inspiration to them" (*Boethian Apocalypse* 100), a suggestion that makes the *Confessio* seem livelier than critics have made it. Wood draws on the *Vox Clamantis* to provide a reading context for *Troilus and Criseyde*, and by his comparisons to the *Vox*, Wood demonstrates that *Troilus* is a serious and moral poem.

Like Chaucer, Gower is acquainted with the Troilus legend and alludes to it in his works (see Olsen, "Defense," for a discussion of Gower's use of the legend). It is a tale which he knows well and expects his audience to know well and which he uses to evoke ideas and images from common medieval culture. He does not, however, retell it at length. In contrast, his versions of other tales provide reading contexts for Chaucer's works that cut through modern misconceptions. One example lies in Gower's treatment of classical heroines, especially in the *Legend of Good Women*. It has long been known that the two works recount the same tales based on the same sources. In 1882, M. Bech studied the influence of the *Legend* on the "Quellen und Plan" (313) of the *Confessio*, and in 1909, G. L. Kittredge pointed out that Gower tells most of the tales in the *Legend* as well as that of Alceste, which Chaucer undoubtedly intended to tell "as the final chapter in his series" (359). Both poets relate the story of Phyllis and Demophon, but their versions are strikingly different. Janet M. Cowen has observed that Chaucer's Demophon is so villainous and his Phyllis so victimized that a reader is given "a low view" (430) of both. In contrast, Robert Worth Frank, Jr., suggests, Gower tells the story as "an example of forgetfulness" (147) in which we sympathize with both parties. The contrast suggests that a comparison of the tales in the *Confessio* and the *Legend* can illuminate the artistry of each. It is curious that discussion of the *Confessio* is seldom used to help us understand interpretative *cruces* in the *Legend*.

Criticism of the *Legend* has suffered from the tendency of critics to construct hypotheses in the absence of facts because they find the *Legend* difficult. Another problem in scholarship on the *Legend* is that critics have tended to be amazed at some of the heroines whom Chaucer includes. Robert Max Garrett, arguing that the Legends are humorously satiric, suggests that Chaucer knew that the tale of Medea "must be carefully expurgated and freed from the stain of child-murder" (68) and that Chaucer expected his audience to appreciate the joke. In her 1983 study of the *Legend*, Lisa J. Kiser argues that the legend of Cleopatra, like that of Medea, provides examples of "dishonest selectivity" which changes women "of bad reputation into paragons of goodness" (100). She states that medieval writers presented Cleopatra and Medea as "examples of satanic lust, unfaithfulness, and other assorted vices" and that Chaucer tries deliberately to "turn the bad into the good" (100-1).

One problem that critics like Garrett and Kiser exemplify is the tendency of modern readers to employ what Greenfield has called the "fallacy of homogeneity" (9) and to "assume a representativeness or orthodoxy of opinion and thought in the intellectual milieu of an age" (Greenfield, 9). Cowen has argued that reading the *Legend* "as a work which functions neatly by doing the opposite of what it professed to do, ... is itself too neat" (433). It is clear that in the works of some medieval writers, classical heroines like Cleopatra and Medea represent vices (see, for example, Root and Taylor). Such is not necessarily the case, because images drawn from classical tales are often pliant[1] and change from the work of one author to another or even between different works by the same author. Kiser notes this fact when she points out that "the basic stories of history and past fiction may pass from 'forme into forme': they are not limited to a single, inviolable shape" (113) even though she expects the stories of Cleopatra and Medea to be "inviolable." Cowen notes that one point which makes the *Legend* different "from the saints' legendary which is its ostensible model is the absence of a uniform point of view. ... The poem is neither pure pathos nor pure satire" (435). The difference comes from the fact that Chaucer regards his materials as pliant. Frank has noted that "in Chaucer's day the *reworking* of classical material ... was an act of preservation and propagation" (13) [italics mine], and I should like to suggest that we should expect to find stories reworked, even in the case of that of Dido, the most important classical heroine found in medieval writings.

Mary Louise Lord has pointed out that modern readers, familiar with Virgil's Dido, are usually surprised that Dido was used by Patristic "Christian writers as a model of chaste widowhood" (22). She points out that "the Apologists ... preferred an older version of the legend to the one used by Vergil" (22). She argues that "it was to the advantage of Christian writers to revive the memory of the faithful Dido and to include her among their examples of chastity and of fortitude. Readers, both pagan and Christian, had to weigh for themselves their choice of the Vergilian or of the chaste Dido. Both traditions flourished, and ... the quarrel between them continued to reverberate for many centuries in Western literature" (44). Craig Kallendorf shows that such reverberation is found in the works of Boccaccio. Boccaccio's "major Latin writings consistently reject the Virgilian account of Dido--the account he had developed earlier in his own *volgare* works--in favor of the 'historical,' chaste queen of Carthage" (Kallendorf, 404) [italics Kallendorf's]. Since Boccaccio treats Dido as a pliant image, it is not surprising that Chaucer does so too. Indeed, Chaucer deliberately manipulates the Virgilian and Ovidian stories to emphasize details which suggest that "in love--and by implication in life as well--one should not make final judgments on the basis of outward appearance" (Hall, 158). Because the *House of Fame* embeds "the Ovidian love story ... in the larger context of Virgilian epic" (Delany, 55), Chaucer shows that "contradictions [are] inherent in the literary tradition" (Erzgräber, 123). As a result, the members of the audience must reassess their interpretation of both Dido and Aeneas.

The situation is complicated by the fact that medieval authors demonstrate ambiguous attitudes to classical authors as well as to the characters represented in classical texts. Frank has shown that there were different views of Ovid in the Middle Ages (see 15). Similarly, medieval authors had divided opinions of other classical authors, as may be exemplified by Boccaccio's dual attitude to Virgil. Furthermore, as James Wimsatt has pointed out, Chaucer tends to compose his poems by making "an entirely new fabric from strands of the work of several writers" ("Sources" 231). As in the case of the story of Alcyone where he changes the Ovidian version by eliminating the metamorphosis (see Burke, "Sources" 13), he often treats works of a single author as pliant. Hiscoe points out that Gower realizes that the tales he retells are well-known and suggests that Gower exploits his audience's familiarity with classical texts in his "manipulation of traditional Ovidian tales" (375) and adaptation of "Ovid's comic strategy to the concerns of a medieval Christian audience" (375). Hiscoe argues that the purpose of the tale of Ceyx and Alcyone in both the

Metamorphoses and medieval versions is "to awaken us to the proper power of love and to our proper natures" (378). Critics often suggest that Chaucer's purpose in the *Book of the Duchess* is to adapt the story of Ceyx and Alcyone so that it provides a parallel for that of the Black Knight because he and his lady "are the modern equivalents of Ceyx and Alcyone" (Fyler, 72). His strategy is the same as that which Hiscoe identifies as Gower's, to make us understand both love and ourselves, even though Chaucer's version is more radically changed from Ovid's than is Gower's.

According to Hiscoe, by treating their inherited Ovidian material as pliant, medieval authors like Gower and Chaucer resemble Ovid, who "metamorphoses myths" so that "the readers' interest in the work is generated not so much by the fictions themselves as by what Ovid does to the familiar stories" (Hiscoe, 369). Hiscoe argues that "the humor in the poem is largely created by the ever-present gap between the stories as the audience would already know them and the versions" Ovid relates (369). He suggests that although Gower's purpose in retelling "a series of self-consciously disfigured myths is not precisely the same as Ovid's, both poets organize their poems around this central comic strategy" (369). I should like to suggest that Hiscoe has isolated both the spirit of Ovidian comedy and the organizing comic strategy of the *Legend* as well as the *Confessio*, for both Gower and Chaucer use a strategy that imitates Ovid's when they "metamorphose" Ovidian tales.

Heroines like Cleopatra and Medea depicted in both the *Confessio* and the *Legend* are pliant figures just as Dido and Alcyone are, and writers like Gower and Chaucer depict them positively in part to force the members of their audience "to weigh for themselves" (Lord, 44) their understanding of the heroines and their relationship to received literary tradition. In particular, the heroines depicted in the *Confessio* help us understand the heroines of the *Legend* without finding it necessary to resort to the imaginary biography of Chaucer as Garrett does. Readers of the *Confessio* have been intrigued by Gower's deliberate "metamorphosis of Ovid's *Metamorphoses*" (Beidler, *Gower's Transformations* v; see also Hiscoe and Wetherbee) and have therefore been more open about Gower's depiction of Cleopatra and Medea than those concerned with the *Legend* have been about Chaucer's. Indeed, Peck speaks respectfully of the fact that Gower "molds the well-known story [of Medea] in unique ways" (109), an action for which Chaucer has often been criticized. As a result, both the *Confessio* and modern studies thereof help us appreciate the *Legend*.

In a study of medieval versions of the legend of Cleopatra, Beverly Taylor argues that "the view of Cleopatra that came to Chaucer from classical sources is invariably unflattering" (250) and that "we can trace in medieval literature a Cleopatra tradition which is wholly consistent with the negative view developed in antiquity" (255-56). In part, however, Taylor makes her point by ignoring some evidence that contradicts her thesis, such as the fact that Cleopatra is "a symbol of faith and constancy in two poems by Lydgate" (Frank, 40), and by interpreting as negative some references to Cleopatra which may not be. She dismisses Gower's Cleopatra as negative by arguing that although the lovers in Book Eight "seem to be celebrated" (258), the fact that the poem concludes when Amans leaves the service of love means that Cleopatra and the other lovers are actually denigrated. This interpretation does a disservice to the literary artistry of the *Confessio*. Diller suggests that Amans' farewell to love is that of an old man but that "the love of young people is explicitly commended" (47). Since Cleopatra represents one of the young lovers in the lovers' paradise, the most probable explanation is that Gower intended her to be a positive figure. Given Gower's serious depiction of the young ladies in the lovers' paradise as positive images and his expressed sympathy for "the wofull queene/ Cleopatras" (VIII, 2572-73) and her "sorwe" (VIII, 2576), I would argue that both Gower and Chaucer wish to persuade the members of the audience to re-examine their reaction to this pliant figure.

Burke has shown that the *Confessio* is unusual because it is marked by "almost total absence of negative female stereotypes and antifeminist propaganda" ("Women" 238) and that Gower deliberately presents women favorably by changing negative depictions in his sources. In her discussion of Medea, she argues that Gower transforms "the character of Medea and of the love between her and Jason" ("Women" 243), a point similar to that of Peck, who suggests that Gower recounts a story which "focuses on personal commitment ... within the larger context of feudal commitments" (109). I believe that examination of Gower's lengthy tale of Medea helps us understand Chaucer's *Legend of Medea*.

Burke analyzes in detail the changes that Gower makes in the versions of the story of Medea inherited from Ovid and Benoît, pointing out that Gower changes specifically "the elements of the story which suggest an *exemplum* of unbridled female passion" ("Women" 246) [italics Burke's]. Although Gower never idealizes Medea, he humanizes her; Peck shows that he makes Medea seem more of "a sensitive girl" (110) than she is in Benoît. When he uses Ovid as his source, he depicts Medea as "an obedient wife" (Peck, 113), thereby engaging the reader's sympathies. Ito also emphasizes that the changes Gower makes are those which present Medea sympathetically, for example, omitting Benoît's description of her beauty in order to focus on "her inward beauty, that is, her devotion for her husband Jason" (*John Gower* 86). Gower also changes the episodes involving Medea's sorcery, omitting her murder of Pelias and making her rejuvenation of Aeson seem natural: her magic is always "used for a good purpose" (Ito, *John Gower* 91). Peck argues that Gower exonerates Medea for the murder of her children by placing the blame on Jason, whose "perjury ... broke the sacred bonds between them" (115).

Chaucer's brief *Legend of Medea* presents the story of Medea more succinctly than Gower's tale does. Robert K. Root notes that "in the Prologue to the *Man of Law's Tale* we are told that any one who will read Chaucer's *Legend* ... may see ... 'the crueltee of thee, queen Medea'" (124) although Chaucer does not depict her murder of her children. Since the *Legend* does not mention Medea's infanticide, I should like to suggest that the Man of Law's reference thereto provides an example of the humor that Sullivan notes in the *Prologue*: just as the Man of Law mentions a detail from the Latin legend of Apollonius of Tyre that Gower does not include, so he mentions a detail from the Latin legend of Medea that Chaucer does not include. As a result, the *Man of Law's Prologue* does not help us interpret the *Legend of Medea*, but Gower's tale of Medea does. Ito suggests that Gower downplays Medea's revenge "to the minimum beyond which both tradition and poetic justice ... would be violated" (*John Gower* 97). Chaucer suppresses even Medea's punishment of Jason, juxtaposing the legend of Medea and that of Hypsipyle; his Jason is "unpunished in spite of his successive betrayals of the two women" (Ito, *John Gower* 94). As a result of his treatment of the pliant figure of Medea, she becomes a suitable figure for the *Legend* because she represents the plight of a woman in a male-centered system of love which says that women must be sweet and passive and that their only revenge for male oppression is--to quote the comment Oliver Goldsmith made several centuries after Chaucer wrote--"to die" (122).

Critics assume that the story of Alceste would have been the last one of the *Legend* (see Frank and Kittredge), but one puzzle of Chaucer scholarship has always been what the nature of that legend would have been. Chaucer treats Alceste as a pliant image just as he treats Dido, Cleopatra, and Medea; Kiser has argued that he "alters the end of the Alcestis story to make even clearer the analogy between her life and the process by which literature discloses meaning" (58). In other words, the accuracy of the story is unimportant in comparison to the purpose the story serves within the *Legend*. Gower refers to Alceste twice in the *Confessio*, once as the heroine of a narrative embedded in the tale of King, Wine, Woman, and Truth in Book Seven and once as one of the ladies in the Lover's Paradise in Book Eight. Burke observes that "Gower's introduction of the tale of Alcestis to offset the example of Apame is not paralleled in any source for the story" and that "the treatment of Alcestis herself is also selective and independent with relation to its probable sources" ("Sources" 11). Burke suggests that Gower makes explicit "the typological parallels with the Virgin Mary and Christ in Alcestis's intercession and death on another's behalf" ("Sources" 13), a point which Gallacher also makes (see 104). When we recall that Chaucer's Alceste also resembles the Virgin Mary (see Kiser, 47-48), we realize that Chaucer's purpose is as serious as

Gower's despite the obvious humor and irony of the *Prologue*'s treatment of Chaucer the protagonist and his encounter with the god of Love. Given the brevity and simplicity of Gower's tale and the way that the material included therein matches the information given about Alceste in the *Prologue*, it is probable that Chaucer's version would have followed similar lines but would have ended with the metamorphosis of Alceste into the daisy, a metamorphosis which would serve to return the *Legend* to the beginning.

The stories of Cleopatra and Medea on the one hand and Alceste on the other represent different ways of handling classical tradition: both Gower and Chaucer depict the former two as good women whereas some authors depict them as evil, and Chaucer invents a new ending for the story of Alceste, whom all authors depict as good. The story of Lucrece represents a third way of handling materials from classical tradition, because she represented "a chaste woman as early as the first century A.D." (Harder, 1). The tradition about Lucrece inherited by the late Middle Ages was not, however, a uniform one, because St. Augustine interpreted her story pejoratively in *De Civitate Dei*, suggesting that her suicide represented her shame lest people think she had consented to the rape willingly (see Book One, Chapter 19). Kiser points out that the narrator of the *Legend* mentions Augustine but then "ignores the substance of Augustine's lengthy commentary on Lucretia's case and attributes to him a feeling of 'gret compassioun' ... for her" (105). I believe that Chaucer mentions Augustine's name for a reason analogous to that for making his statements in the *House of Fame* that one who wishes to learn about Dido should "rede Virgile in Eneydos/ Or the Epistle of Ovyde" (Chaucer, 285: 378-79) and in the *Legend* that he takes "in Naso and Eneydos .../ The tenor" (Chaucer, 500: 928-29): to call attention to discrepancies in the inherited tradition and remind the members of his audience that classical heroines are pliant figures who can be depicted in different ways. In contrast to Chaucer, Gower uses Livy and Ovid (see Harder, 3), both of whom praise Lucrece, and ignores the contradictory Augustinian tradition, although the fact that he identifies the rapist as Aruns rather than Sextus raises problems concerning both his sources and his purpose in the tale of Lucrece. Carol Weiher has argued that Chaucer "uses the sinfulness of men to point up his real concern, the heroine's virtue" (9) whereas Gower emphasizes Aruns in order to discuss chastity as "the fifth point of policy a king must follow" (9); the authors' treatments of the pliant classical tale are appropriate to the purposes of the works.

Weiher points out that Gower tells the tales of Lucretia and Virginia as a pair and that "Chaucer's Physician's Tale was meant to be the companion of the tale of Lucretia in the *Legend of Good Women*" (7). This fact raises the question of the relationship of the *Confessio* to Chaucer's most popular work, the *Canterbury Tales*. A good approach to the subject lies in a consideration of the way in which the two poets handle the tale of Virginia. Like Alceste, Virginia is a heroine who is treated positively in both classical and medieval sources, and like Chaucer's Lucrece, his Virginia is treated pathetically. Weiher points out that Gower and Chaucer modify their sources in different ways but "ultimately achieve the same result: Lucretia and Virginia stories that closely resemble one another" (7). Gower exploits the similarity between the stories by juxtaposing them as two of the last three tales in Book Seven, which concludes with the tale of Tobias and Sara whose emphasis is on "love" (VII, 5321) and "lawe and kinde" (VII, 5363). He tells both without the sentimentality that marks Chaucer's versions.

Frank has argued that "Chaucer created a very characteristic pattern in his pathetic tales. Helplessness, innocence, suffering, and grief are the principle elements" (95). This pattern exists in Chaucer's version of a story both he and Gower retell which does not involve a classical heroine but which likewise shows the attitude of both poets to what the *Legend* calls "these olde appreved stories" (Chaucer, 483: 21). In this case, the story is that of Constance, whose source is medieval rather than classical, Trivet's *Anglo-Norman Chronicle*. It is a commonplace of modern criticism that the *Man of Law's Tale* is a work which displays "superb craftsmanship" (Block, 572) and that Chaucer's version provides a contrast to "the simpler versions of Trivet and Gower" (Schlauch, 161). More recent scholars have re-evaluated the versions, and it is clear from their research that Chaucer and Gower each treat the pliant image of Constance in a way that is appropriate for inclusion in the context in which each uses it. Paul Theiner observes that the Man of Law takes "every opportunity to make the relatively simple story he inherited into romance, parable, sentimental story, and saint's life all rolled into one, with asides on morality, piety, astrology, and poverty, as well as countless ironic comments on his inability to keep the story going without bluster and delay" (179). My summary of Theiner's argument is that Chaucer adapts the pliant tale of Constance to suit its place in the tale-telling game that is the *Canterbury Tales* (see 170). A similar point is made by Joseph E. Grennen, who suggests that the *Man of Law's Tale* is "a lawyer's account of the sufferings of a woman who is the very embodiment of the virtue of *constantia*" ("Chaucer's Man of Law" 498) [italics Grennen's].

Gower's purpose in retelling the tale of Constance is different from that of Chaucer, and his version "lacks the sentimental and agitated persona" (Peck, 63) of Chaucer's although he adapts Trivet's narrative no less carefully to its context in the *Confessio* than Chaucer does to its context in the *Canterbury Tales*. Gallacher points out that Constance's "remarkable odyssey dramatizes the spiritual and temporal triumph of good reputation ... over the evil of detraction" (102), a point applicable to Gower's discussion of the sin of Envy in Book Two. Ito calls Gower's "manner of narration" "matter-of-course" (*John Gower* 28), and I believe that Gower has simplified his narration to make it fit the context. The tale is an example of the branch of Envy "which cleped is Detraccioun" (II, 387), which occurs when a person is unwilling to speak "a plein good word withoute frounce" (II, 392). It is therefore appropriate that Gower tell the tale with "plein good words." Although the tale is fairly long (1,012 lines in length), Gower uses only two puns therein, one of which I discussed in chapter three: "And fro this worldes faierie/ [God] hath take hire into compaignie" (II, 1593-94). The other is the statement that Moris "was abandouned/ To Cristes feith" (II, 1596-97), in which "abandouned" means both "given up" and "devoted," contextually appropriate to the story of a child abandoned by his father and saved by the grace of God the Father, to Whom he is afterwards devoted. Since the tale of Constance ends at l. 1598, it is noteworthy that Gower uses the only puns of the tale near the end, almost as a signal that this plainly told tale is approaching its conclusion and that subsequent tales will be told in Gower's customary metonymic poetic style, including the frequent use of puns.

In the tale of Constance, however, Gower uses "rimes équivoques" as he does throughout the *Confessio*. In the tale of Florent, there are eighteen "rimes équivoques" in a 455-line tale (4% of the couplets); in the tale of Constance, there are forty-five in a 1,012-line tale, for a comparable proportion of 4.4%. In contrast to his usual practice, however, Gower seems to avoid using "rimes équivoques" in this tale whenever possible. The first time that he uses the heroine's name, "Constance" (II, 620) in a rhyming position, he calls attention to the importance of the heroine and the virtue of constancy by rhyming "Constance" (II, 620) with "circumstance" (II, 619). Thereafter, he rhymes "Constance" (II, 678, 1375, 1446, and 1520) with "ordinance" (II, 677), "resemblance" (II, 1376), "chance" (II, 1445), and "remembrance" (II, 1519), and he once uses a variant form of the name, "Custe" (II, 1219), which rhymes with "Saluste" (II, 1220).

In the tale of Constance, Gower tends to avoid using many of the "rimes équivoques" that he uses throughout the *Confessio*. In a tale which emphasizes the importance of Christian faith, it is surprising to find the rhyme of "wise" [manner] and "wise" [wise] occurring only once: "And over that in such a wise/ Sche hath hem with hire wordes wise" (II, 605-6). Its position in the nineteenth and twentieth lines of the tale, however, does emphasize its importance. In a similar way, considering that the tale emphasizes Constance's sea voyages and the mutability of human life associated therewith, it is surprising that Gower uses the "rime équivoque" on "schipe" and "-schipe" only twice. The first occurs on her arrival in "Northumberlond" (II, 717) when Elda's people "out of the *Schip* with gret *worschipe/* ... tok hire into *felaschipe*" (II, 741-42) [italics mine] and the second when the "renegat" (II, 1093) named "Theloüs" (II, 1092) "withoute *felaschipe/* Hath take a bot and cam to *Schipe*" (II, 1107-8) [italics mine]. Because the first passage occurs as Constance finds a safe haven and the second as she finds a dangerous one, the "rimes équivoques" do not evoke the theme of the Sea Voyage as they do in the tale of Appolinus.

In contrast to the tale of Appolinus, in which Gower rhymes "betide" (VIII, 1788) with "tyde" (VIII, 1787) [ocean tide] in order to evoke metonymically the themes of the Sea Voyage and the Providence of God, in the tale of Constance, he rhymes "betide" (II, 1105) with "tide" (II, 1106) [time]: "Thus sche lai,/ Unknowe what hire schal *betide*;/ And fell so that be nyhtes *tide*/ This knyht withoute felaschipe/ Hath take a bot and cam to Schipe" (II, 1104-8) [italics mine]. The four lines are one of the few examples in the tale of Constance of a cluster, a device which Gower frequently uses to call attention to important ideas, and the rhyme of "betide" and "tide" is followed by the rhyme of "felaschipe" and "Schipe." I should like to suggest, therefore, that Gower deliberately avoided using "tyde" [ocean tide] in the rhyming position in order to avoid evoking the theme of the Sea Voyage. Although Gower rhymes "mariage" (II, 625) with "corage" (II, 626), he uses no metonymic web about proper human relationships within the tale, an idea linked to the Sea Voyage in other contexts. It seems probable that Gower uses "rime équivoque" in the tale of Constance to emphasize that his words are "plein" and "good" rather than to pun.

Despite the fact that Gower uses many fewer puns in the tale of Constance than he does in the *Confessio* as a whole and that he uses "rime équivoque" differently than he does in other tales or in the frame narrative, the presence of puns and "rime équivoque" remind us that the tale is told with conscious literary artistry. It is, basically, a matter of taste whether a reader prefers the sentimental, pathetic version of Chaucer's *Man of Law's Tale* or the spare narrative of Gower's tale of Constance. It is well for the literary critic to remember George Orwell's observation that "when one critic writes, 'The outstanding feature of Mr. X's work is its living quality,' while another writes, 'The immediately striking thing about Mr. X's work is its peculiar deadness,' the reader accepts this as a simple difference of opinion" (162).

Readers must decide for themselves whether they prefer Gower's or Chaucer's versions of the tale of Pyramus and Thisbe, the Ovidian source of which Chaucer followed closely, whereas Gower paraphrased it (see Macaulay's discussion, Gower, vol. I: 497). They must also decide whether they prefer Chaucer's *Wife of Bath's Tale* or Gower's tale of Florent, unbiased by the conventional critical interpretation that the former is poetically superior to the latter. Fischer notes that the *Wife of Bath's Tale* uses dialogue that leads to a high "proportion of suspense and drama, vividness and intensity" (216). Although Fischer concludes that Gower's poetry is "dull"--or at best "soothing" and "harmonious" in comparison to "the sprightliness and raciness of Chaucer's verse" (225)--many of her observations indicate the high level of linguistic artistry of the tale of Florent. She points out, for example, that Gower uses "complex and interwoven sentences" (213), a rhetorical tactic that one may well prefer to the choppier sentence structures used by Chaucer. Furthermore, as I have shown in chapters three and four, Gower's use of puns and "rimes équivoques" makes the tale of Florent and the *Confessio* as a whole anything but dull.

A comparison of the *Wife of Bath's Tale* and the tale of Florent on the level of linguistic and literary artistry indicates that both poets provide examples of medieval poetic artistry although they differ from one another. As Hiscoe observes, one who appreciates the way that Gower manipulates his "comic strategy through the hundreds of tales in [the] *Confessio Amantis* can also begin to appreciate why the medieval audience that valued Chaucer both for his moral teachings and his humor considered John Gower his equal" (382). This insight provides a point of departure for a discussion of the relationship of one of the most puzzling of the *Canterbury Tales*, the *Manciple's Tale*, to the *Confessio Amantis*. This relationship has been obscured in part by misinterpretation of the *Manciple's Tale* and in part by the "Chaucer legend" and the denigration of Gower which has traditionally accompanied it.

In an article published in 1963, Richard Hazelton argued that the *Manciple's Tale* is a "parody and critique" (1) of Gower's tale of Phebus and the Crow and of the "narrative method in the *Confessio Amantis*" (22). Hazelton represents the school of critics who assume that Chaucer was a greater literary artist than Gower and that he enjoyed calling attention to the fact, an assumption questioned by Sullivan in 1953 in respect to the *Man of Law's Prologue*. Hazelton argues that to "overlook the deft play of the parodist's craft is to be left with the *common reader's Chaucer*" (31) [italics mine], suggesting thereby that those with different views of both Chaucer and Gower somehow lack critical acumen. F. N. M. Diekstra points out, however, that "if one looks closely at the features of Chaucer's style that Hazelton adduces to suggest Chaucer's parodying of Gower's style one finds that they are all features that Chaucer used elsewhere as well, where any relevance to Gower's practice is out of the question" (147), a fact which helps us discount Hazelton's interpretation.

One problem with Hazelton's study is that he assumes that Chaucer's main source for the *Manciple's Tale* is the *Confessio Amantis*, although it is based on Ovid and possibly also on the *Ovide Moralisé* and "Machaut's *Voir Dit* or some French or English fabliau version" (Diekstra, 131). Chaucer's version of the tale of Phebus and the Crow is marked by a treatment of the pliant classical sources reminiscent of that in other tales by both Chaucer and Gower. William Askins points out that "the Manciple himself ... indicates clearly that he has taken liberties with the Ovidian tradition" (91) and suggests that Chaucer treats his Ovidian material as a pliant text in order to make it serve a new literary purpose.

Recent criticism, although not denying the humor of the *Manciple's Tale*, has shown that it is serious and "reflects some of Chaucer's deepest considerations about the nature of his art" (Traversi, 142). Such criticism contrasts to Hazelton's stricture that reading the *Tale* seriously "is to assume that the piece is a tract and not a work of comic art" (31). Many critics have overemphasized the "comic art" of the *Canterbury Tales* at the expense of its didactic effect. It seems that the present is an appropriate time to go what Gower calls "the middel weie" (Pro., 17) and recapture the seriousness of the *Tales* as well as their humor. Wood, for example, argues that "confession is not only important for a study of Gower but for the *Canterbury Tales* as well, since the Parson's meditation on penance, which closes the *Tales*, is in its way a kind of confessional manual, preparing the pilgrims for the confession they would be expected to make upon their arrival at Canterbury" ("Speech" 216). He suggests that "the good pedagogical and religious uses of speech in his [the Parson's] tale may be contrasted with the slanderous and self-serving uses of speech in the *Manciple's Prologue* and *Tale*" ("Speech" 216).

There is a more subtle relationship between the *Manciple's Tale* and the *Confessio* than has usually been noticed, and both Gower and Chaucer are using the same classical stories in different but equally pliant ways to investigate subjects of interest to both. Before considering the relationship between the *Manciple's Tale* and the *Confessio*, one must realize that Gower's tale of Phebus and Cornide is of greater literary artistry than has usually been granted. Diekstra argues that "the fact that the raven is the mistress's pet, not Phoebus' as in the other versions, reduces any regret we may have felt for the bird's fate" (135). His brief discussion suggests the care with which Gower has adapted his inherited materials despite the fact that the tale is only thirty-five lines long. The care is also shown by the fact that the physical change of the crow from "whyt" (III, 797) to "colblak" (III, 808) is paralleled by the metamorphosis of his name from "Corvus" (III, 796) to "Raven" (III, 812).

I should like to point out that the Gowerian analogue to the *Manciple's Tale* is broader than the tale of Phebus and Cornide alone. The *Manciple's Tale* also incorporates another story that Gower tells in Book Three of the *Confessio*, the tale of Alexander and the Pirate. Wood notes that the Manciple's "gratuitous insults to the Cook surely indicate strife in the heart" ("Speech" 217) and that the Parson's discussion of Wrath includes chiding, "the sin that characterizes the Manciple" ("Speech" 218). Since the sin of Wrath characterizes the Manciple's performance in his *Prologue*, it is not surprising that his tale should interweave two brief tales that Gower tells separately in Book Three, whose subject is Wrath. This fact suggests, not that Chaucer wished to parody Gower, but that both poets shared common interests and modified their inherited materials in different ways but for similar purposes.

This brief comparison of the works of Gower and Chaucer has suggested that the poets are more similar than has usually been granted and that they are governed by the same "metalinguistic consciousness" which they incorporate into their "strategies of composition" (Vance, 294). In particular, both poets are concerned with language on all levels, from the smallest levels of dictional choice and appropriateness of tales to their narrators to the largest levels of the choice of stories to relate and concern about the interpretations their audiences might make of those stories. By manipulating pliant figures from both the classical and the medieval traditions, both poets make their audiences responsible for understanding the poems and reacting to them in the best way possible. The end of the *Confessio* seems to say farewell to poetry in words which echo Chaucer's in his late "Lenvoy de Chaucer a Scogan," "In no rym, dowteles,/ Ne thynke I never of slep to wake my muse" (Chaucer, 539: 37-38):

> My muse doth me forto wite,
> And seith it schal be for my beste
> From this day forth to take reste,
> That y nomore of love make.
> (VIII, 3140-43)

In their completed forms, the literary works of both poets are committed to the reader to interpret and appreciate, with an understanding of the linguistic and literary context in which both poets composed.

Conclusion

Frank has argued that many modern readers find Gower displeasing because "our expectations from a 'long read' are oriented toward the epic, for sweep or for progressive complexity. A series of tales in a medieval collection makes no such claims" (172). I would add that in the twentieth century, the problem is compounded by the fact that readers are used to the novel and evolutionary fiction. Frank suggests that we can only appreciate a work like the *Confessio Amantis* when we understand both the form and "what a particular writer sets out to do with the form" (172-73). I have argued throughout this study that the techniques developed by structuralist critics help us understand both the form of the *Confessio* and the specific use to which Gower puts that form.

Jonathan Culler states that the existence of a poem means that "certain possibilities exist within the tradition; it is written in relation to other poems ... [and] presupposes conventions of reading which the author may work against, which he can transform, but which are the conditions of possibility of his discourse" (30). Structuralism, therefore, is a technique that "seek[s] the system behind the event, the constitutive conventions behind any individual act" (Culler, 30), in the case of literary criticism, the conventions that underlie a specific literary work. Because structuralism helps us understand the system that underlies particular events, that is, in this case, the form of the *Confessio* and its many large and small constituent parts, we as readers are free to appreciate the literary artistry of the *Confessio* in a way that those who come to it with misapprehensions of its nature cannot do.

Culler argues that "to discover and characterize structures one must analyze the system which assigns structural descriptions to the objects in question" (120). In order to "formulat[e] ... the internalized competence which enables objects to have the properties they do for those who have mastered the system" (Culler, 120), we must adjust our expectations of what Frank calls "a 'long read'" (172) to acquire the ability to appreciate a medieval story collection like the *Confessio*. In the first chapter of this study, I have suggested that a profitable way to achieve such "competence" is to understand one structural analogue of the *Confessio*. Hiscoe's juxtaposition of the *Confessio* and Ovid's *Metamorphoses* helps show that Gower is not humorless as many critics assume. In the same spirit, I have juxtaposed the *Confessio* to a work which is an analogue to it and therefore provides clues that help our interpretation of it: Dante's *Vita Nuova*. The comparison helps us appreciate the humor of the *Confessio* (albeit from a different angle than Hiscoe's comparison to the *Metamorphoses* provides) as well as Gower's serious treatment of the theme of love.

Culler notes that genres are "sets of expectations which allow sentences of a language to become signs of different kinds in a second-order literary system" (129). Thus, although the first necessity is to understand the genre of the *Confessio* as well as possible because our understanding thereof governs our understanding of the entire poem and its parts, it is also necessary to study both the sentences of which the *Confessio* is composed and the narrative units which can be understood by their analogy to the model of the sentence. In the second chapter of this study, I have argued that we must be aware of the interrelationships between the parts of the *Confessio* in order to appreciate the literary artistry of the components of the poem.

Culler observes that structuralism should attempt "to develop an esthetics based on the pleasure of the reader" (263), and an appreciation of the artistry of the large rhetorical structures of the *Confessio* frees us to examine the aesthetics of the poem at the linguistic level. In chapters three and four, I have discussed the puns and "rimes équivoques" of the *Confessio* in order to show the artistry of Gower's sensitivity to and use of language. In chapter five, I have argued that appreciation of the *Confessio* depends on understanding the way in which some of the literary structures derive from the native English oral-formulaic tradition. Since "there are crucial differences between the conventions of oral communication and those of literature" (Culler, 133), it is imperative that one interested in the aesthetics of the *Confessio* understand the conventions that derive from oral rather than written poetry. A true appreciation of the aesthetics of the *Confessio*, not only shows Gower's literary artistry, but also helps us appreciate literature written in Ricardian England (and specifically the works of Chaucer discussed in chapter six) in a new way. Culler argues that the value of structuralist poetics is that it makes explicit "what is implicitly known by all those sufficiently concerned with literature to be interested in poetics" (258). A structuralist interpretation of the *Confessio Amantis* has a somewhat broader purpose: to make explicit what was implicitly known by readers of the first few centuries after the composition of the *Confessio*, that the *Confessio* is a work well worth reading for its clear plot lines and beautiful metonymic poetry.

Notes

Preface

1. See Fisher's discussion of "the denigration of Gower's character which accompanied the Chaucer legend" (24) and his survey of the adverse albeit influential judgments passed on Gower by literary critics. For a survey of Gower's early reputation and of the fact that for two centuries after his death he was "given equal respect if not equal admiration" (Gilroy-Scott, 30) in comparison to that given to Chaucer, see N. W. Gilroy-Scott, who studies literary allusions to the works of Gower, and Pearsall, "Gower Tradition."

2. A useful survey of recent scholarship about the works of Gower that shows the changing opinions about his literary artistry is Yeager's "The Poetry of John Gower."

3. George D. Economou has defined historical scholarship as that "approach that seeks to illuminate the work of art by applying to our interpretation of it as much relevant information as is available about the original period of the work--its social, political, artistic, intellectual, and religious conventions and traditions" (6).

4. In a study that speaks of modern criticism of Old English poetry, Fred C. Robinson makes a comment applicable to the study of Middle English texts as well, pointing out that "books and articles claimed to be based on 'a study of the literary texts themselves' undistracted by historical, paleographical, or linguistic matters" (66) often produce "bizarre and arbitrary 'critical readings'" (67). Such readings are the Scylla that a modern reader must avoid while at the same time avoiding the Charybdis of interpreting texts in so narrowly "historical" a manner that they seem of no interest to modern readers.

Chapter One

1. In this chapter, I am arguing that the *Vita Nuova* is a work which shares many features with the *Confessio Amantis* and that a comparison of the two works illuminates both the genre and certain structural features of the *Confessio*. Although it is irresistible to speculate that it may have been the source, a critic would have to be able to prove two things: that Gower was familiar with Dante's poetry and that the *Vita* was known in fourteenth-century England. The question of whether he was familiar with Dante has

never been answered authoritatively, although many assume that Gower had no knowledge of Italian poetry (see Mossé, 314). Gower's only reference to Dante mentions "how Dante the poete answerde/ To a flatour" (VII, 2329*-30*), and the Latin gloss to the passage says, "Nota exemplum cuiusdam poete de Ytalia, qui Dante vocabatur" (vol. II: 296) [Mark this example of a certain poet of Italy who was named Dante]. Because the reference is to Dante the man rather than to his works, it is easy to assume that Gower knew the name but not the works (see Toynbee). Albert S. Cook argues that Gower may have known the *De Monarchia* (see 395), and Macaulay suggests that the passage about Envy that Gower attributes to Seneca may actually be based on *Inferno* 13: 64 (see Gower, vol. I: 491). If true, this fact would indicate that Gower was familiar with the *Commedia*. Leonard has argued that "the course of action in Gower's poem is loosely analogous to that in the *Divine Comedy*" (63) and that "in its cure for love, ... [the] *Confessio Amantis* more nearly resembles the *Divine Comedy* than the *Roman de la Rose*" (63). Although Leonard does not claim that the *Commedia* directly influenced the *Confessio*, her argument that "both Dante and Gower were working in the same mode with the same materials and that many of the same attitudes obtain in their poems" (64) raises the intriguing possibility that Gower imitated Dante.

The question of the influence of Dante on Gower is part of a larger question, that of the possible influence of Dante on Middle English poets in general, which many critics deny existed. Indeed, as Leonard points out, "some Chaucer scholars even question whether Chaucer 'really knew' Dante's poems" (64), although others are convinced that he did so. Gower belonged to the same circle as did Chaucer, and he would presumably have had access to the same intellectual ideas as Chaucer. Recent work on Chaucer has shown that he came into contact with Italian circles while involved with the City of London and the Court (see Childs, 66-67, and Schless, 195), especially while working in customs. Furthermore, it has shown that "Chaucer lived in a society where international contacts were a commonplace of commercial, diplomatic, religious, and intellectual life. Links with France, Flanders and Spain were strong in his age, but many Englishmen in his circle would also have been to Italy, or have friends and relatives who had been there, or would know Italians in England" (Childs, 84). Wendy Childs has argued that Chaucer's contacts may have "prepared him for Italy's new literature" (84), as they may also have prepared Gower, who refers to "hem that duelle among ous here,/ Of suche as we Lombardes calle" (II, 2100-1).

Even in the case of Chaucer, it is impossible to determine where he learned Italian or if he knew it, because Italian merchants and nobles spoke French and officials Latin (see Larner, 18), and he may have read Italian literature in French translation. It is also impossible to determine authoritatively which works by Italian authors Middle English poets knew; for example, it is clear that Chaucer read and used Tractate IV [of the *Convivio*] and the *canzone* that prefaces it, ... but there is so far no conclusive evidence that he knew the first three Tractates" (Boitani, "What Dante Meant" 130) [italics Boitani's]. Roberta Payne has recently argued that it is probable that Chaucer knew the *Vita*. This idea is rendered especially reasonable by the fact that Boccaccio's *Il Filostrato*--Chaucer's source for *Troilus and Criseyde*--contains echoes of the *Vita* (see Wood, *Elements* 6). Given the circles in which Gower as well as Chaucer lived and worked, and given the fairly widespread knowledge of Dante in fourteenth-century England (evidenced, for example, by the *Pearl* poet and by a monk named Adam Easton, who knew Dante's work and bequeathed his books "to his home monastery at Norwich" [Childs, 78]), it is possible that Gower was familiar with Dante. Recent scholars have suggested that fourteenth-century England shared more with Renaissance Italy than earlier scholars believed (see Coleman, 49), and there is a humanist dimension to Gower's work which might have made him interested in Italian authors. For example, "among the characteristics that are frequently cited as evidence of a humanist movement is the development of the mirror-for-princes genre" (Coleman, 60), and both the *Vox* and the *Confessio* are in part of that genre. Coleman defines it as a "handbook of advice for monarchs or republics" ("English Culture" 60). Gower originally called the *Confessio* the former ("a bok for king Richardes sake" [Pro., 24*]) and changed it to the latter ("a bok for Engelondes sake" [Pro., 24]). One cannot prove beyond a shadow of doubt that Gower was acquainted with Italian literature, although the suggestion seems tenable, at the least an intriguing albeit unprovable possibility. In the absence of irrefutable proof that Gower knew Dante's work and that the *Vita Nuova* was known in England, all one can say is that the *Vita* and the *Confessio* are of the same literary genre and share structural characteristics and that a comparison of the two illuminates the *Confessio*.

2. Gower's choice of English for the main language of the *Confessio* represents a stance between "earnest" and "game." In his study of Chaucer's *Troilus*, Vance points out that "it is safe to venture that, at a time when the several tongues of Europe had become emblems of new political entities, Chaucer's project of writing Troy's story 'out of Latyn in my tonge' was no empty ideological gesture" because Chaucer was suggesting "that his culture was not only heir to, but perhaps even a rival with, the revered classical 'auctors' of the past" (302). Gower's use of English to write a book "for king Richardes sake" (Pro., 24*) or "for Engelondes sake" (Pro., 24) likewise represents both a linguistic "ideological gesture" and a desire to promote the "lust" of his poem.

3. Colin Hardie notes that "Singleton's interpretation [of chapter twenty-five of the *Vita*] has not carried conviction with the reviewers" (32), and he argues that Dante "inserted the chapter ... without seeing how inadequate to his whole story, indeed how destructive of it, his rather elementary piece on the rhetorical doctrine of personification ... was" (32). Hardie thus suggests, without directly saying so, that Dante is a lesser literary artist than most readers believe; critics have frequently charged that Gower's works lack literary artistry, citing reasons similar to those Hardie cites in respect to Dante.

4. Wimsatt points out that "dream poems did not constitute a separate category of love narratives" (*Chaucer* 125) in the Middle Ages. The *Confessio*, which Constance B. Hieatt argues may have been intended to be interpreted as a dream vision (see *Realism* 47), is of the type Wimsatt calls a "waking vision" (*Chaucer* 125) because no actual dream takes place. Leonard compares the *Confessio* to the *Commedia*, arguing that there is "a remarkable similarity between the ways in which Dante and Gower establish the dream quality of their poems. Rather than falling asleep, the Dreamer awakens; that is, he suddenly perceives his existence on earth as a sleep and a forgetting that leads to the death of the soul. The dream into which he wakes is designed to teach him the way to righteousness. ... Without saying literally that Amans goes to sleep and awakens into a dream, Gower makes the dream structure effective in his poem by his references to waking at both the beginning and the end of his confession" (81). In a persuasive argument, Howard suggests that the *Canterbury Tales* is recounted by a narrator whose "memory becomes a wellspring of narrative" (143) and that it is a Book of Memory analogous to the *Vita Nuova* (see 142). I am making a similar point in respect to the *Confessio*.

5. Cherniss points out that "Gower uses the word 'charite' as a synonym for this 'love' in the Prologue, ... and he returns to 'thilke love which ... stant of charite confermed' at the very end of the poem" (*Boethian Apocalypse* 105).

Chapter Two

1. For a survey of scholarship on the frame and encapsulated narratives of the *Confessio*, see Yeager, *John Gower Materials* and "The Poetry of John Gower." There are also a number of studies of what might be called extra-literary matters, of which two of the most valuable are Jeremy Griffith's review of the illustrated manuscripts of the *Confessio*, which casts light on questions of manuscript transmission, and Kate Harris' argument that "bad

texts ... provide the earliest true criticism of the *Confessio*" and "information on the history of poetics" (40).

2. A student of literature must use structuralist techniques with care because the methodologies were not developed for literary analysis. As Brewer points out, "linguistics is not literary criticism, but literary critics may deny themselves valuable insights, knowledge and concepts if they disregard the work of their colleagues on the nature of language, the conditioning medium of literature" ("Some Metonymic Relationships" 41).

3. Katharine A. Gittes has argued that Gower fragments the story of Ulysses deliberately in order to depict him as a representative of "the Christian soul as silent rhetorician" (7). Her essay suggests that the structural units of the *Confessio* differ from those of the tales when we consider them as tales.

4. By the late fourteenth century, "pite" had become an ambiguous word. Stevens argues that Chaucer "was occupied in his *Canterbury Tales* romances with 'the civilization of the heart'; and their motto might well be his own favorite line--'For pitee renneth soone in gentil herte'" (50). Other critics, however, have detected irony and even satire in Chaucer's use of the line, especially in the *Merchant's Tale*. Gower uses the term in its courtly and theological senses with no ironic glances at the nature of pity in a fallen world.

Chapter Three

1. I should like to thank my colleague Professor Raymond P. Tripp, Jr., who is studying the literary effect of puns in *Beowulf*, for bringing these studies to my attention. I should also like to thank Professor Elizabeth Robertson of the University of Colorado for suggesting that Maureen Quilligan's *The Language of Allegory* provides insights helpful to sudying the literary effect of puns in Middle English poetry.

2. Brown suggests that a pun "possesses a semi-metaphoric status" (17). However, as Muir points out, puns provide "an illogical reinforcement of the logical sequence of thought" ("Uncomic Pun" 483) in a literary work; I should like to suggest that their literary effect is metonymic rather than "semi-metaphoric." Despite this difference of terminology, I have adopted many of Brown's insights and much of his terminology in this study.

3. Although I interpret the poem as a secular lyric, I derived the idea that

"beste" is a pun meaning both "best" and "beast" from Reiss, and I use his edition of the lyric (18).

4. In a study of the metaphor of the bridle in *Anelida and Arcite*, D. Gillam points out that the metaphor "offers an appropriate vehicle for signalling who holds the *maistrie* in a heterosexual relationship" (395); she does not, however, discuss the pun implicit in the use of bridle/ bridall.

5. A portion of this chapter has appeared as "The Literary Impact of the Pun in Middle English Poetry." Although the lists of puns included in chapters three and four are quite lengthy, they are necessary to suggest the frequency with which Gower puns in the *Confessio*. When puns occur infrequently in a literary work, it is always possible that they are merely an aspect of the English language. Gower uses a large number of puns and puns of all the types identified by linguistic scholars, and they are clearly an important part of his literary technique. An appreciation thereof heightens our appreciation of the artistry of the *Confessio*.

Chapter Four

1. The critic interested in the literary effect of punning rhymes runs into the same problems as the critic interested in the literary effect of puns in general: "The metalinguistic vocabulary for forms of speech play is not as precise as careful analysis would require" (Sherzer, 347). As a result, there is no general agreement about the terminology to use to describe Gower's punning rhymes. Kate Harris differentiates between "rime riche," which she defines as "rhyme of initial, stem and terminal" like Gower's "rhyming on 'acord' and 'discord'" (37), "'rime équivoque' (that is, rhyme on homonyms)" (37), "'rime contrefaite' (rhyme on homophones)" (37), and "'meilleurs rimes' ... [which] act as a form of punctuation" (37). Critics like Ito and Burrow do not make such a distinction. I use the general term "rime équivoque" because it seems to capture the essence of Gower's punning rhymes. My discussion focuses on the literary effect of the rhymes rather than on sub-categories thereof.

2. There also exist a tenth-century scholastic metrical version full of "scholarly words and expressions" and a "brief rhythmical poem in ... the *Carmina Burana*" (Kortekaas, 5). The former "consists of 792 Leonine hexameters in the shape of a dialogue" (Kortekaas, 151), and the latter seems to be "written in an individual, contemplative style" (Kortekaas, 154). I have not considered these poetic versions because they seem to have

been unknown to Gower.

3. S. Singer, the most recent editor of Gotfried's *Pantheon*, prints the riddle found in the Latin prose, noting, "findet sich in *C5*, da es aber in *C2* und *D3* fehlt, gehört es doch wol nicht V^1 an, sondern ist durch glossierung hereingekommen" (Gotfried, 154) [italics Singer's].

4. Gower's use of the rhymes of "while" and "wel" act in a manner that is reminiscent of the rhetorical "envelope patterns" of Old English poetry. Adeline C. Bartlett identified the "envelope pattern" as "any logically unified group of verses bound together by repetition at the end of (1) words or (2) ideas or (3) words and ideas which are employed at the beginning" (9). Hieatt shows that envelope patterns can bracket longer passages than those identified by Bartlett. The *Andreas* poet, for example, brackets a passage of great thematic importance by an exact repetition of a formula in ll. 595 and 811. On the assumption that Hieatt is correct to argue that the envelope pattern "is an important rhetorical device arising out of the formulaic nature of oral poetry ... inherited by later poets whose work was unquestionably literate" ("Envelope Patterns" 256), I have adopted this useful concept to describe the way that Gower's repetition of particular "rimes équivoques" works, even though the rhetorical envelopes that I perceive in the *Confessio* are substantially larger than those Hieatt identifies in *Andreas*.

Chapter Five

1. I should like to thank my colleague Professor Raymond P. Tripp, Jr., for calling my attention to the fact that the pun on "beste" resembles that on "dēore."

2. This chapter is an adaptation of my "Literary Artistry and the Oral-Formulaic Tradition."

3. Although Frederick W. Moorman suggested in 1905 that a storm in the *Troy Book* was probably based "on actual acquaintance with ... [Old English] poetry" (77), recent scholars discount the possibility for the logical reason that there is no evidence that Old English manuscripts were read during the Middle English period. Nicholas Jacobs compares the poems and their sources "to determine how far the English storm-descriptions are the work of the English poets, and thus how far a topos may be said to exist in English at all" (695). Jacobs attributes the passages to "Latin literary models" (713) rather than to English oral tradition, and he alludes only in

passing to the *Confessio* (see 713).

4. When Lewis comments that Gower's line "Up to the Sky he caste his lok" (VIII, 1928) might have "come from Homer" (207), he apparently perceives the relationship between Gower's poetry and oral-formulaic poetry without being aware of the fact. He does not, however, develop the comparison.

5. Apollonius' departure from Pentapolim is found in the Latin versions, but not in the Old English *Apollonius*, which consists of two eleventh-century fragments, the beginning and end of the story. Since the narrative "has been well reproduced in a pleasing Old English idiom" (Goolden, *Old English "Apollonius"* xxiii), a reader has pragmatic reasons for assuming that the missing section resembled the Latin. Whenever I discuss only the Latin rather than the Latin and Old English texts, the reader should be aware that there is no Old English version of that passage.

6. There are numerous extant manuscripts of the Latin prose *Apollonius* and numerous variants among different recensions. For example, "the two principle versions RA and RB [differ] in a linguistic and stylistic respect: RA is verbose, in a Latin that is somewhat vulgar in tone, RB on the contrary is characterized by a tendency to classical terseness" (Kortekaas, 61). Because "major differences in content occur very seldom" (Kortekaas, 61), and because, as Macaulay points out, Gower seems to have used both Gotfried's *Pantheon* and a recension of the Latin prose (see Gower, vol. II: 537), it is unlikely that scholars will be able to identify authoritatively the prose text that Gower used. Peter Goolden has argued that the Latin notes in the margin of the passage including Antiochus' riddle suggest that Gower used a "corrupt text" ("Antiochus's Riddle" 247) of the tale of Appolinus, a version that "agrees with several of the Latin manuscripts" ("Antiochus's Riddle" 247) and with the Old English version; he does not, however, speculate about which extant version may have been Gower's source. Because the text of RB is linguistically superior to that of RA, I have chosen to quote from it, unless RA includes illuminating phrases not in RB; in the latter case, I quote from both versions.

7. Cynewulf uses the type-scene at the end of *Juliana* as part of his depiction of the death and damnation of the villain Heliseus, who is responsible for Juliana's martyrdom. In *Juliana*, however, heroic concepts play "a basically negative" role, because Cynewulf uses them "in such a way that they become the secular concepts and inadequate values against which the Christian concepts and values work" (Cherniss, *Ingeld and Christ* 194). As a result, Cynewulf depicts Heliseus as a villainous figure in part because he is heroic, a more subtle characterization than that of Taliart in

the Latin *Apollonius*, whose author does not intend to invert a traditional heroic image.

Chapter Six

I. Gower's interest in the pliancy of classical tales is especially pertinent if we grant the argument that Christopher Ricks makes from the point of view of one who likes Gower but is not a medievalist: that Gower favors the use of words which "have in common a high degree of plasticity such as is altogether germane to Gower's supreme concern: metamorphosis" (28). Ricks suggests that Gower uses lexical items in a way similar to that in which I perceive medieval poets to have used classical tales.

Works Cited

Askins, William. "The Historical Setting of *The Manciple's Tale*." *Studies in the Age of Chaucer* 7 (1985): 87-105.
Audiau, Jean. *Les Troubadours et L'Angleterre: Contribution à l'Étude des Poètes Anglais de l'Amour au Moyen-Age (XIIIe et XIVe Siècles)*. Paris: Librarie Philosophique J. Vrin, 1927.
Augustine (S. Aurelii Augustini). *De Civitate Dei Libri XXII*, 2 vols., ed. B. Dombart and A. Kalb. Leipzig: Teubner, 1928-29.

Baum, Paull F. "Chaucer's Puns." *PMLA* 71 (1956): 225-46.
- - -. "Chaucer's Puns: A Supplementary List." *PMLA* 73 (1958): 167-70.
Bech, M. "Quellen und Plan der 'Legende of Goode Women' und ihr Verhältniss zur 'Confessio Amantis'." *Anglia* 5 (1882): 313-82.
Beidler, Peter G., ed. *John Gower's Literary Transformations in the "Confessio Amantis": Original Articles and Translations*. Washington, D.C.: Univ. Press of America, 1982.
- - -. "The Tale of Acteon." In *John Gower's Literary Transformations in the "Confessio Amantis": Original Articles and Translations*, ed. Peter G. Beidler. Washington, D.C.: Univ. Press of America, 1982, 7-10.
Bennett, J. A. W. "Gower's 'Honeste Love'." In *Patterns of Love and Courtesy: Essays in Memory of C. S. Lewis*, ed. John Lawlor. Evanston: Northwestern Univ. Press, 1966, 107-21.
Block, Edward A. "Originality, Controlling Purpose, and Craftsmanship in Chaucer's *Man of Law's Tale*." *PMLA* 68 (1953): 572-616.
Boitani, Piero. *English Medieval Narrative in the Thirteenth and Fourteenth Centuries*, trans. Joan Krakover Hall. Cambridge: Cambridge Univ. Press, 1982.
- - -. "What Dante Meant to Chaucer." In *Chaucer and the Italian Trecento*, ed. Piero Boitani. Cambridge: Cambridge Univ. Press, 1983, 115-39.
Braddy, Haldeen. "The Genre of Chaucer's *Squire's Tale*." *JEGP* 41 (1972): 279-90.
Braswell, Mary Flowers. *The Medieval Sinner: Characterization and Confession in the Literature of the English Middle Ages*. Rutherford: Fairleigh Dickinson Univ. Press, 1983.
Brewer, Derek. "Some Metonymic Relationships in Chaucer's Poetry." *Poetica* (Tokyo) 1 (1974): 1-20. Rpt. in *Chaucer: The Poet as Storyteller*. London: The Macmillan Press, 1984, 37-53.
- - -. "Towards a Chaucerian Poetic." *PBA* 60 (1974): 219-52. Rpt. in *Chaucer: The Poet as Storyteller*. London: The Macmillan Press, 1984, 54-79.

Brown, James. "Eight Types of Puns." *PMLA* 71 (1956): 14-26.
Burch, J. C. Horton. "Notes on the Language of John Gower." *ES* 16 (1934): 209-15.
Burke, Linda Barney. "The Sources and Significance of the 'Tale of King, Wine, Woman and Truth' in John Gower's *Confessio Amantis*." *Greyfriar: Siena Studies in Literature* 21 (1980): 3-15.
- - -. "Women in John Gower's *Confessio Amantis*." *Mediaevalia* 3 (1977): 238-59.
Burrow, John A. "The Portrayal of Amans in *Confessio Amantis*." In *Gower's "Confessio Amantis": Responses and Reassessments*, ed. Alastair J. Minnis. Cambridge: D. S. Brewer, 1983, 5-24.
- - -. *Ricardian Poetry: Chaucer, Gower, Langland, and the "Gawain" Poet*. London: Routledge and Kegan Paul, 1971.

Calin, William. "Defense and Illustration of *Fin'Amor*: Some Polemical Comments on the Robertsonian Approach." In *The Expansion and Transformations of Courtly Literature*, ed. Nathaniel B. Smith and Joseph T. Snow. Athens: The Univ. of Georgia Press, 1980, 32-48.
Carson, M. Angela. "Easing of the 'Hert' in the *Book of the Duchess*." *Chaucer Review* 1 (1966): 157-60.
Casson, Leslie F. "Studies in the Diction of the *Confessio Amantis*." *Englische Studien* 69 (1934): 184-207.
Cawley, A. C., ed. *Secunda Pastorum*. In *The Wakefield Pageants in the Townley Cycle*. Old and Middle English Texts. Manchester: Manchester Univ. Press, 1958, 43-63.
Chaucer, Geoffrey. *Works*. 2nd. Edn., ed. F. N. Robinson. Boston: Houghton Mifflin Co., 1961.
Cherniss, Michael D. *Boethian Apocalypse: Studies in Middle English Vision Poetry*. Norman, OK: Pilgrim Books, 1987.
- - -. *Ingeld and Christ: Heroic Concepts and Values in Old English Christian Poetry*. The Hague: Mouton, 1972.
Childs, Wendy. "Anglo-Italian Contacts in the Fourteenth Century." In *Chaucer and the Italian Trecento*, ed. Piero Boitani. Cambridge: Cambridge Univ. Press, 1983, 65-87.
Chrétien de Troyes. *Cligés*. In *Christian von Troyes: Sämtliche Werke*, vol. 1, ed. Wendelin Foerster. Halle: Max Niemeyer, 1884, 1-353.
Coleman, Janet. "English Culture in the Fourteenth Century." In *Chaucer and the Italian Trecento*, ed. Piero Boitani. Cambridge: Cambridge Univ. Press, 1983, 33-63.
Cook, Albert S. "Dante and Gower." *Archiv für das Studium der neuren Sprachen und Literaturen* 132 (1914): 395.
Cooper, Helen. *The Structure of the Canterbury Tales*. Athens: The Univ.

of Georgia Press, 1984.
Cowen, Janet M. "Chaucer's *Legend of Good Women*: Structure and Tone." *SP* 82 (1985): 416-36.
Cowling, Samuel T. "Gower's Ironic Self-Portrait in the *Confessio Amantis*." *AM* 16 (1975): 63-70.
Crowne, David K. "The Hero on the Beach: An Example of Composition by Theme in Anglo-Saxon Poetry." *NM* 61 (1960): 362-72.
Culler, Jonathan. *Structuralist Poetics*: *Structuralism, Linguistics, and the Study of Literature*. Ithaca, N.Y.: Cornell Univ. Press, 1975.

Dante Alighieri. *Vita Nuova Rime*, ed. Fredi Chiapelli. GUM, n.s. vol 7. Milan: U. Mursia and Co., 1973.
David, Alfred. "The Man of Law vs. Chaucer: A Case in Poetics." *PMLA* 82 (1967): 217-25.
Dean, James. "Time Past and Time Present in Chaucer's Clerk's Tale and Gower's *Confessio Amantis*." *ELH* 44 (1977): 401-18.
Delany, Sheila. *Chaucer's "House of Fame"*: *The Poetics of Skeptical Fideism*. Chicago: The Univ. of Chicago Press, 1972.
Diekstra, F. N. M. "Chaucer's Digressive Mode and the Moral of *The Manciple's Tale*." *Neophilologus* 67 (1983): 131-48.
Diller, Hans-Jürgen. "'For Engelondes sake': Richard II and Henry of Lancaster as Intended Readers of Gower's *Confessio Amantis*." In *Functions of Literature*: *Essays Presented to Erwin Wolff on His Sixtieth Birthday*, ed. Ulrich Broich, Theo Stemmler, and Gerd Stratmann. Tübingen: Max Niemeyer Verlag, 1984, 39-53.
Dorfman, Eugene. *The Narreme in the Medieval Romance Epic*: *An Introduction to Narrative Structures*. Univ. of Toronto Romance Series, vol. 13. Toronto: Univ. of Toronto Press, 1969.
Dragonetti, Roger. *La Vie de la Lettre au Moyen Age*: *"Le Conte du Graal."* Paris: Éditions du Seuil, 1980.

Economou, George D. "Introduction: Chaucer the Innovator." In *Geoffrey Chaucer*: *A Collection of Original Articles*, ed. George D. Economou. New York: McGraw-Hill Book Co., 1975, 1-14.
Erzgräber, Willi. "Problems of Oral and Written Transmission as Reflected in Chaucer's *House of Fame*." In *Historical and Editorial Studies in Medieval and Early Modern English, for Johan Gerritsen*, ed. Mary-Jo Arn, Hanneke Wirtjes, and Hans Jansen. Groningen: Wolters-Noordhoff, 1985, 113-28.
Esch, Arno. "John Gowers Erzählkunst." In *Chaucer und seine Zeit*: *Symposium für Walter F. Schirmer*, ed. Arno Esch. Tübingen: Max

Niemeyer Verlag, 1969, 207-39.

Farnham, Anthony E. "The Art of High Prosaic Seriousness: John Gower as Didactic Raconteur." In *The Learned and the Lewed: Studies in Chaucer and Medieval Literature*, ed. Larry D. Benson. Harvard English Studies, vol. 5. Cambridge, Mass.: Harvard Univ. Press, 1974, 161-73.

Fischer, Olga C. M. "Gower's *Tale of Florent* and Chaucer's *Wife of Bath's Tale*: A Stylistic Comparison." *ES* 66 (1985): 205-25.

Fisher, John H. *John Gower: Moral Philosopher and Friend of Chaucer*. New York: New York Univ. Press, 1964.

Foley, John Miles. "*Beowulf*: Oral Tradition Behind the Manuscript." In *Approaches to Teaching "Beowulf*," ed. Jess B. Bessinger, Jr., and Robert F. Yeager. Approaches to Teaching Masterpieces of World Literature, vol. 4. New York: The Modern Language Association of America, 1984, 130-38.

- - -. "Formula and Theme in Old English Poetry." In *Oral Literature and the Formula*, ed. Benjamin A. Stolz and Richard S. Shannon, III. Ann Arbor: Center for the Coördination of Ancient and Modern Studies, 1976, 207-32.

- - -. "The Oral Theory in Context." In *Oral Traditional Literature: A Festschrift for Albert Bates Lord*, ed. John Miles Foley. Columbus, Ohio: Slavica Publishers, Inc., 1981, 27-122.

Frank, Robert Worth, Jr. *Chaucer and "The Legend of Good Women."* Cambridge, Mass.: Harvard Univ. Press, 1972.

French, Walter Hoyt and Charles Brockway Hale, ed. *King Horn*. In *Middle English Metrical Romances*, vol. 1. New York: Russell and Russell, Inc., 1964, 25-70.

Fyler, John M. *Chaucer and Ovid*. New Haven: Yale Univ. Press, 1979.

Gallacher, Patrick J. *Love, the Word, and Mercury: A Reading of John Gower's "Confessio Amantis."* Albuquerque: Univ. of New Mexico Press, 1975.

Ganshof, F. L. *Feudalism*, trans. P. Grierson. New York: Harper and Row, 1964.

Garrett, Robert Max. "'Cleopatra the Martyr' and her Sisters." *JEGP* 22 (1923): 64-74.

Gillam, D. "Lovers and Riders in Chaucer's 'Anelida and Arcite'." *ES* 63 (1982): 394-401.

Gilroy-Scott, N. W. "John Gower's Reputation: Literary Allusions from the Early Fifteenth Century to the Time of 'Pericles'." *Yearbook of English Studies* 1 (1971): 30-47.

Gittes, Katherine S. "Ulysses in Gower's *Confessio Amantis*: The Christian

Soul as Silent Rhetorician." *ELN* 24, no. 2 (December, 1986): 7-14.
Glasser, Marc. "'He Nedes Moste Hire Wedde': The Forced Marriage in the *Wife of Bath's Tale* and Its Middle English Analogues." *NM* 85 (1984): 239-41.
Goldsmith, Oliver. *The Vicar of Wakefield*. In *The Vicar of Wakefield and Miscellaneous Works*. New York: The American News Co., 1890, 1-178.
Goodall, Peter. "John Gower's *Apollonius of Tyre*: *Confessio Amantis*, Book VIII." *Southern Review: Literary and Interdisciplinary Essays* 15 (1982): 243-53.
Goolden, Peter. "Antiochus's Riddle in Gower and Shakespeare." *RES*, n.s. 6 (1955): 245-51.
- - -, ed. *The Old English "Apollonius of Tyre."* Oxford: Oxford Univ. Press, 1958.
Gotfried von Viterbo. *Pantheon*. In *Apollonius von Tyrus: Untersuchungen über das Fortleben des antiken Romans in spätern Zeiten*, ed. S. Singer. Halle, a.S.: Max Niemeyer, 1895, 150-77.
Gower, John. *Balade XX*. In *The Complete Works of John Gower, vol. I: The French Works*, ed. G. C. Macaulay. Oxford: The Clarendon Press, 1899, 354-55.
- - -. *The English Works*, ed. G. C. Macaulay. 2 vols. EETS, e.s. 81 and 82. London: Oxford Univ. Press, 1969.
- - -. *Mirour de l'Omme*. In *The Complete Works of John Gower, vol. I: The French Works*, ed. G. C. Macaulay. Oxford: The Clarendon Press, 1899, 3-334.
- - -. *Vox Clamantis*. In *The Complete Works of John Gower, vol. 4: The Latin Works*, ed. G. C. Macaulay. Oxford: The Clarendon Press, 1902, 1-344.
Gray, Douglas. "Later Poetry: The Courtly Tradition." In *The Middle Ages*, ed. W. F. Bolton. Sphere History of Literature in the English Language, vol. 1. London: Barrie and Jenkins, 1970, 312-70.
Greenfield, Stanley B. *The Interpretation of Old English Poems*. London: Routledge and Kegan Paul, 1972.
Grennen, Joseph E. "Chaucer's Man of Law and the Constancy of Justice." *JEGP* 84 (1985): 498-514.
- - -. "*Hert-huntyng* in the *Book of the Duchess*." *MLQ* 25 (1964): 131-39.
Griffiths, Jeremy. "*Confessio Amantis*: The Poem and Its Pictures." In *Gower's "Confessio Amantis": Responses and Reassessments*, ed. Alastair J. Minnis. Cambridge: D. S. Brewer, 1983, 163-78.

Hall, Louis Brewer. "Chaucer and the Dido-and-Aeneas Story." *MS* 25 (1963): 148-59.

Harder, Henry L. "Livy in Gower's and Chaucer's Lucrece Stories." *Publications of the Missouri Philological Assn.* 2 (1977): 1-7.
Hardie, Colin. "Dante and the Tradition of Courtly Love." In *Patterns of Love and Courtesy: Essays in Memory of C. S. Lewis*, ed. John Lawlor. Evanston: Northwestern Univ. Press, 1966, 26-44.
Harrington, David V. "The Harley Lyric *Wynter Wakeneth Al My Care*." *The Explicator* 44 (1986): 3-4.
Harris, Anne Leslie. "Hands, Helms, and Heroes: The Role of Proper Names in 'Beowulf'." *NM* 83 (1982): 414-21.
Harris, Kate. "John Gower's *Confessio Amantis*: The Virtues of Bad Texts." In *Manuscripts and Readers in Fifteenth-Century England: The Literary Implications of Manuscript Study*, ed. Derek Pearsall. Cambridge: D. S. Brewer, 1983, 27-40.
Hazelton, Richard. "The *Manciple's Tale*: Parody and Critique." *JEGP* 62 (1963): 1-31.
Heller, L. G. "Toward a General Typology of the Pun." *Language and Style* 7 (1974): 271-82.
Hieatt, Constance. "On Envelope Patterns (Ancient and--Relatively--Modern) and Nonce Formulas." In *Comparative Research on Oral Traditions: A Memorial for Milman Parry*, ed. John Miles Foley. Columbus, Ohio: Slavica Publishers, Inc., 1987, 245-58.
- - -. *The Realism of Dream-Visions: The Poetic Exploitation of the Dream-Experience in Chaucer and His Contemporaries*. De Proprietatibus Litterarum, Series Practica, vol. 2. The Hague: Mouton, 1967.
Hill, Archibald A. "Structural Evidence on the Reality of Literary Punning." In *Studies in Diachronic, Synchronic, and Typological Linguistics, Festschrift for Oswald Szemerenyi: On the Occasion of his 65th Birthday*, Part 1. Amsterdam: John Benjamin B.V., 1979, 373-85.
Hiscoe, David W. "The Ovidian Comic Strategy of Gower's *Confessio Amantis*." *PQ* 64 (1985): 367-85.
Höfer, Paul. *Alliteration bei Gower*. Leipzig-Reudnitz: Druck von Oswald Schmidt, 1890.
Howard, Donald R. *The Idea of the Canterbury Tales*. Berkeley: Univ. of California Press, 1976.
Huppé, Bernard F. "*Petrus Id Est Christus*: Word-Play in *Piers Plowman*, the B-text." *ELH* 17 (1950): 163-90.

Irving, Edward B., Jr. *A Reading of "Beowulf."* New Haven: Yale Univ. Press, 1968.
Ito, Masayoshi. "Gower's Use of *Rime Riche* in *Confessio Amantis*--As Compared with his Practice in *Mirour de l'Omme* and with the Case of Chaucer." *Studies in English Literature* 46 (1969): 29-44.

- - -. *John Gower: The Medieval Poet*. Tokyo: Shinozaki Shorin, 1976.

Jacobs, Nicolas. "Alliterative Storms: A Topos in Middle English." *Speculum* 47 (1972): 695-719.
Jakobson, Roman. "Two Aspects of Language: Metaphor and Metonymy." In *Fundamentals of Language*, by Roman Jakobson and Morris Halle. Janua Linguarum, vol. 1. 'S-Gravenhage: Mouton and Co., 1956, 76-82. Rpt. in *European Literary Theory and Practice: From Existential Phenomenology to Structuralism*, ed. Vernon W. Gras. New York: Dell Publishing Co., 1973, 119-29.
Kallendorf, Craig. "Boccaccio's Dido and the Rhetorical Criticism of Virgil's *Aeneid*." *SP* 82 (1985): 401-15.
Kaplan, Theodore H. "Gower's Vocabulary." *JEGP* 31 (1932): 395-402.
Kean, Patricia M. *Chaucer and the Making of English Poetry*. 2 vols. London: Routledge and Kegan Paul, 1972.
Kellogg, A. L. "Chaucer's Self-Portrait and Dante's." *MÆ* 29 (1960): 119-20.
Kelly, L. G. "Punning and the Linguistic Sign." *Linguistics* 66 (1971): 5-11.
Kinneavy, Gerald. "Gower's *Confessio Amantis* and the Penitentials." *Chaucer Review* 19 (1984): 144-61.
Kirk, Elizabeth D. "Chaucer and His English Contemporaries." In *Geoffrey Chaucer: A Collection of Original Articles*, ed. George D. Economou. New York: McGraw-Hill Book Co., 1975, 111-27.
Kiser, Lisa J. *Telling Classical Tales: Chaucer and the "Legend of Good Women."* Ithaca: Cornell Univ. Press, 1983.
Kittredge, G. L. "Chaucer's *Medea* and the Date of the *Legend of Good Women*." *PMLA* 17 (1909): 343-63.
Klaeber, Friedrich, ed. "*Beowulf*" and "*The Fight at Finnsburg*." 3rd edn. with 1st and 2nd Supplements. Boston: D. C. Heath and Co., 1950.
Kökertiz, Helge. "Rhetorical Word-Play in Chaucer." *PMLA* 69 (1954): 937-52.
Koestler, Arthur. *The Act of Creation*. New York: MacMillan, 1964. 6th Edn. 1967.
Kortekaas, G. A. A., ed. *Historia Apollonii Regis Tyri*. Mediaevalia Groningana, vol. 3. Groningen: Bouma's Boekhuis, 1984.

Langland, William. *The Vision of Piers Plowman: A Complete Edition of the B-text*, ed. A. V. C. Schmidt. London: J. M. Dent and Sons, Ltd.; New York: E. P. Dutton and Co., Inc., 1978.
Langlois, M. E., ed. *Recueil d'Arts de Seconde Rhétorique*. Collection de Documents Inédits sur l'Histoire de France. Paris: Imprimerie

Nationale, 1902.
Larner, John. "Chaucer's Italy." In *Chaucer and the Italian Trecento*, ed. Piero Boitani. Cambridge: Cambridge Univ. Press, 1983, 7-32.
Lawlor, John. "On Romanticism in the 'Confessio Amantis'." In *Patterns of Love and Courtesy: Essays in Memory of C. S. Lewis*, ed. John Lawlor. Evanston: Northwestern Univ. Press, 1966, 122-40.
Leonard, Frances McNeely. *Laughter in the Courts of Love: Comedy in Allegory, from Chaucer to Spenser*. Norman, OK.: Pilgrim Books, 1981.
Lewis, C. S. *The Allegory of Love*. New York: Oxford Univ. Press, 1958. 11th Printing, 1967.
Lord, Mary Louise. "Dido as an Example of Chastity: The Influence of Example Literature." *Harvard Library Bulletin* 17 (1969): 22-44 and 216-32.

Manly, John Matthews. "On the Question of the Portuguese Translation of Gower's *Confessio Amantis*." *MP* 27 (1930): 467-72.
Means, Michael H. *The Consolatio Genre in Medieval English Literature*. Gainesville: Univ. of Florida Press, 1972.
Miller, Paul. "John Gower, Satiric Poet." In *Gower's "Confessio Amantis": Responses and Reassessments*, ed. Alastair J. Minnis. Cambridge: D. S. Brewer, 1983, 79-105.
Minnis, Alastair J. "Introduction." In *Gower's "Confessio Amantis": Responses and Reassessments*, ed. Alastair J. Minnis. Cambridge: D. S. Brewer, 1983, 1-4.
- - -. "'Moral Gower' and Medieval Literary Theory." In *Gower's "Confessio Amantis": Responses and Reassessments*, ed. Alastair J. Minnis. Cambridge: D. S. Brewer, 1983, 50-78.
Moorman, Frederick W. *The Interpretation of Nature in English Poetry from "Beowulf" to Shakespeare*. Quellen und Forschungen zur Sprach- und Culturgeschichte der Germanischen Völker, vol. 95. Strassburg: Karl J. Trübner, 1905.
Moser, Thomas C., Jr. "'And I Mon Waxe Wod': The Middle English 'Foweles in the Frith'." *PMLA* 102 (1987): 326-37.
Mossé, Fernand. *A Handbook of Middle English*, trans. James A. Walker. Baltimore: The Johns Hopkins Press, 1952.
Muir, Kenneth. "Shakespeare and Rhetoric." *Shakespeare Jahrbuch* 90 (1952): 49-68.
- - -. "The Uncomic Pun." *The Cambridge Journal* 3 (1950): 472-85.
Musa, Mark, trans. *Dante's "Vita Nuova": A Translation and an Essay*. Bloomington: Indiana Univ. Press, 1973.

Nash, Walter. *The Language of Humor*. English Language Series, vol. 16.

London: Longman, 1985.
OED. *The Compact Edition of the Oxford English Dictionary, Complete Text Reproduced Micrographically.* 2 vols. Oxford: The Univ. Press, 1971.
Olsen, Alexandra Hennessey. "In Defense of Diomede." *In Geardagum* 8 (1987): 1-12.
- - -. "Literary Artistry and the Oral-Formulaic Tradition: The Case of Gower's *Appolinus of Tyre*." In *Current Research on Oral Literature: A Memorial for Milman Parry*, ed. John Miles Foley. Columbus, Ohio: Slavica Publishers, 1987, 493-509.
- - -. "The Literary Impact of the Pun in Middle English Poetry." *In Geardagum* 7 (1986): 17-36.
Olsson, Kurt O. "The Cardinal Virtues and the Structure of John Gower's *Speculum Meditantis*." *The Journal of Medieval and Renaissance Studies* 7 (1977): 113-48.
- - -. "Rhetoric, John Gower, and the Late Medieval *Exemplum*." *M&H* n.s. 8 (1977): 185-200.
Ong, Walter J. "Wit and Mystery: A Revaluation in Mediaeval Latin Hymnody." *Speculum* 22 (1947): 310-41.
Orwell, George. "Politics and the English Language." In *A Collection of Essays*. New York: Harcourt Brace Jovanovich, Inc., 1953, 156-71.
Owst, G. R. *Literature and Pulpit in Medieval England, A Neglected Chapter in the History of English Letters and of the English People.* New York: Barnes and Noble, Inc., 1961.

Parks, Ward. "The Oral-Formulaic Theory in Middle English Studies," *Oral Tradition* 1 (1986): 693-94.
Parry, Milman. "A Comparative Study of Diction as One of the Elements of Style in Early Greek Epic Poetry." In *The Making of Homeric Verse: The Collected Papers of Milman Parry*, ed. Adam Parry. Oxford: The Clarendon Press, 1971, 421-36.
Payne, Roberta L. *The Influence of Dante on Medieval English Dream Visions.* American Univ. Studies, Series II: Romance Languages and Literature, vol. 63. New York: Peter Lang Publishing, Inc., 1989.
Pearsall, Derek. "The Gower Tradition." In *Gower's "Confessio Amantis": Responses and Reassessments*, ed. Alastair J. Minnis. Cambridge: D. S. Brewer, 1983, 179-97.
- - -. "Gower's Narrative Art." *PMLA* 81 (1966): 475-84.
Peck, Russell A. *Kingship and Common Profit in Gower's "Confessio Amantis."* Literary Structures, ed. John Gardner. Carbondale:

Southern Illinois Univ. Press, 1978.
Phelan, Walter S. "Beyond the Concordance: Semantic and Mythic Structures in Gower's Tale of Florent." *Neophilologus* 61 (1977): 461-79.
Prior, Sandra Pierson. "*Routhe* and *Hert-Huntyng* in the *Book of the Duchess*." *JEGP* 85 (1986): 3-19.
Propp, Vladimir. *Morphology of the Folktale*, trans. Laurence Scott. American Folklore Society Bibliographical and Special Series, vol. 9. Indiana Univ. Research Center in Anthropology, Folklore and Linguistics, publication 10. Austin: Univ. of Texas Press, 1968. 5th Printing, 1975.

Quilligan, Maureen. *The Language of Allegory: Defining the Genre*. Ithaca: Cornell Univ. Press, 1979.
Quinn, William A. and Audley S. Hall. *Jongleur: A Modified Theory of Oral Improvisation and Its Effects on the Performance and Transmission of Middle English Romance*. Washington, D. C.: Univ. Press of America, 1982.

Ramsey, Lee C. "The Sea Voyages in *Beowulf*." *NM* 72 (1971): 51-59.
Ransom, Daniel J. *Poets at Play: Irony and Parody in "The Harley Lyrics*." Norman, OK.: Pilgrim Books, 1985.
Reiss, Edmund. *The Art of the Middle English Lyric: Essays in Criticism*. Athens: Univ. of Georgia Press, 1972.
Renoir, Alain. "Crist Ihesu's Beasts of Battle: A Note on Oral-Formulaic Theme Survival." *Neophilologus* 60 (1976): 455-59.
- - -. "The Inept Lover and the Reluctant Mistress: Remarks on Sexual Inefficiency in Medieval Literature." In *Chaucerian Problems and Perspectives: Essays Presented to Paul E. Beichner, C.S.C.*, ed. Edward Vasta and Zacharias P. Thundy. Notre Dame: Notre Dame Univ. Press, 1979, 180-206.
- - -. "Oral-Formulaic Theme Survival: A Possible Instance in the 'Nibelungenlied'." *NM* 65 (1964): 70-75.
Robert de Blois. *Ensoignement des Princes et d'Autres Genz Communemant*. In *Robert de Blois: Son Oeuvre Didactique et Narrative*, ed. John Howard Fox. Paris: Librairie Nizet, 1950, 93-132.
Robinson, Fred C. "Anglo-Saxon Studies: Present State and Future Prospects." *Mediaevalia* 1 (1975): 62-77.
Root, Robert K. "Chaucer's Legend of Medea." *PMLA* 24 (1909): 124-53.
Rowland, Beryl. "The Horse and Rider Figure in Chaucer's Works." *Univ. of Toronto Quarterly* 35 (1965): 246-59.
Runacres, Charles. "Art and Ethics in the *Exempla* of *Confessio Amantis*."

In *Gower's "Confessio Amantis": Responses and Reassessments*, ed. Alastair J. Minnnis. Cambridge: D. S. Brewer, 1983, 106-34.

Russell, P. E. "Robert Payn and Juan de Cuenca, Translators of Gower's *Confessio Amantis*." *MÆ* 30 (1961): 26-32.

Ryan, William M. *William Langland*. TEAS, vol. 66. New York: Twayne Publishers, Inc., 1968.

- - -. "Word Play in Some Old English Homilies and a Late Middle English Poem." In *Studies in Language, Literature, and Culture of the Middle Ages and Later*, ed. E. Bagby Atwood and Archibald A. Hill. Austin: Univ. of Texas Press, 1969, 265-78.

Sacks, Harvey. "On Some Puns: With Some Intimations." In *Sociolinguistics: Current Trends and Prospects*, ed. Roger W. Shuy. Georgetown Univ. Monograph Series on Languages and Linguistics, vol. 25. Washington, D. C.: Georgetown Univ. Press, 1973, 135-44.

Schaar, Claes. "Old Texts and Ambiguity." *ES* 46 (1965): 157-65.

Schlauch, Margaret. "*The Man of Law's Tale*: Introduction." In *Sources and Analogues of Chaucer's "Canterbury Tales*," ed. W. F. Bryan and Germaine Dempster. New York: Humanities Press, 1958, 155-61.

Schless, Howard. "Transformations: Chaucer's Use of Italian." In *Geoffrey Chaucer*, ed. Derek Brewer. Writers and their Background. Athens, Ohio: Ohio Univ. Press, 1975, 184-223.

Schueler, Donald G. "Some Comments on the Structure of John Gower's *Confessio Amantis*." In *Explorations of Literature*, ed. Rima Drell Reck. Louisiana State Univ. Studies: Humanities Series, vol. 18. Baton Rouge: Louisiana State Univ. Press, 1966, 15-24 and 169-70.

Shakespeare, William. *Hamlet*. Ed. Edward Hubler. New York: New American Library, 1963.

Shaw, Judith Davis. "An Etymology of the Middle English *Coise*." *ELN* 22 (1985): 11-13.

- - -. "*Lust* and *Lore* in Gower and Chaucer." *Chaucer Review* 19 (1984): 110-22.

Sherzer, Joel. "Oh! That's a Pun and I Didn't Mean It." *Semiotica* 22 (1978): 335-50.

Singleton, Charles S. *An Essay on the "Vita Nuova*." Cambridge, Mass.: Harvard Univ. Press, 1958.

Smallwood, T. M. "Chaucer's Distinctive Digressions." *SP* 82 (1985): 437-49.

Stevens, John. *Medieval Romance: Themes and Approaches*. London: Hutchinson Univ. Library, 1973.

Stockton, Eric W., trans. *The Major Latin Works of John Gower: The Voice of One Crying and the Tripartite Chronicle.* Seattle: Univ. of Washington Press, 1962.
Stokes, Myra. "The Embarcation of the Hero: A Topos and Its Use in *Patience.*" *Poetica* (Tokyo) 21-22 (1985): 1-24.
- - -. "Recurring Rhymes in *Troilus and Criseyde.*" *SN* 52 (1980): 287-97.
Sullivan, William L. "Chaucer's Man of Law as Literary Critic." *MLN* 68 (1953): 1-8.

Taylor, Beverly. "The Medieval Cleopatra: The Classical and Medieval Tradition of Chaucer's *Legend of Cleopatra.*" *The Journal of Medieval and Renaissance Studies* 7 (1977): 249-69.
Theiner, Paul. "The Man of Law Tells His Tale." *Studies in Medieval Culture* 5 (1975): 173-79.
Thorpe, Lewis. "A Source of the 'Confessio Amantis'." *MLR* 43 (1948): 175-81.
Tiller, Terence, trans. *Confessio Amantis (The Lover's Shrift).* The Penguin Classics, vol. L128. Baltimore: Penguin Books, 1963.
Todorov, Tzvetan. *Grammaire du Décaméron.* Approaches to Semiotics, vol. 3. The Hague: Mouton, 1969.
Topsfield, L. T. *Chrétien de Troyes: A Study of the Arthurian Romances.* Cambridge: Cambridge Univ. Press, 1981.
Toynbee, Paget. *Dante in English Literature from Chaucer to Cary*, vol. 1. London: Methuen and Co., 1909.
Traversi, Derek. *The Literary Imagination: Studies in Dante, Chaucer, and Shakespeare.* Newark: Univ. of Delaware Press, 1982.
Tristram, Hildegard L. C. "Intertextuelle *Puns* in *Piers Plowman.*" *NM* 84 (1983): 182-91.

Utley, Francis Lee. "The Seven Deadly Sins--Then and Now." *Indiana Social Studies Quarterly* 25 (1972): 31-50.

Vance, Eugene. "Mervelous Signals: Poetics, Sign Theory, and Politics in Chaucer's *Troilus.*" *NLH* 10 (1979): 293--337.

Weiher, Carol. "Chaucer's and Gower's Stories of Lucretia and Virginia." *ELN* 14 (1976): 7-9.
Weinberg, Carole, ed. *John Gower: Selected Poetry.* Manchester: Carcanet New Press, Ltd., 1983.
Weiss, Alexander. *Chaucer's Native Heritage.* American Univ. Studies, Series IV, vol. 11. New York: Peter Lang, 1985.
Wetherbee, Winthrop. "Genius and Interpretation in the 'Confessio Amantis'." In *Magister Regis: Studies in Honor of Robert Earl*

Kaske, ed. Arthur Groos. New York: Fordham Univ. Press, 1986, 241-60.
Wickert, Maria. *Studies in John Gower*, trans., Robert J. Meindl. Washington, D.C.: Univ. Press of America, Inc., 1981.
Wimsatt, James. *Chaucer and the French Love Poets*: *The Literary Background of the "Book of the Duchess."* North Carolina Univ. Studies in Comparative Literature, vol. 43. Chapel Hill: The Univ. of North Carolina Press, 1968.
- - -. "The Sources of Chaucer's 'Seys and Alcyone'." *MÆ* 36 (1967): 231-41.
Wittig, Susan. *Stylistic and Narrative Structures in the Middle English Romances*. Austin: Univ. of Texas Press, 1978.
Wood, Chauncey. *The Elements of Chaucer's "Troilus."* Durham, N.C.: Duke Univ. Press, 1984.
- - -. "Speech, the Principle of Contraries, and Chaucer's Tales of the Manciple and the Parson." *Mediaevalia* 6 (1980): 209-29.
Woolf, Rosemary. "Moral Chaucer and Kindly Gower." In *J. R. R. Tolkien, Scholar and Storyteller*: *Essays "In Memoriam,"* ed. Mary Salu and Robert T. Farrell. Ithaca: Cornell Univ. Press, 1979, 221-45.

Yeager, R. F. "Aspects of Gluttony in Chaucer and Gower." *SP* 81 (1984): 42-55.
- - -. *John Gower Materials*: *A Bibliography Through 1979*. Garland Reference Library of the Humanities, vol. 266. New York: Garland Publishing, Inc., 1981.
- - -. "'oure englisshe' and Everyone's Latin: The *Fasciculus Morum* and Gower's *Confessio Amantis*." *SAR* 4 (1981): 41-53.
- - -. "The Poetry of John Gower: Important Studies, 1960-1983." In *Fifteenth-Century Studies*: *Recent Essays*, ed. Robert F. Yeager. Hamden, Conn.: Archon Books, 1984, 3-28.

Index

Amans 7-17, 20, 21-27, 43, 49-50, 56, 58, 66
Book of Memory 16, 108
Chaucer, Geoffrey 1-2, 7, 19, 22, 33-34, 53-55, 71, 87-88, 105, 108; *Anelida and Arcite* 110; *The Book of the Duchess* 40-41, 92; *The Canterbury Tales* 2, 20, 87, 96, 108; *Franklin's Tale* 29; *Manciple's Prologue* 100-1; *Manciple's Tale* 99-100; *Man of Law's Prologue* 88, 94, 99; *Man of Law's Tale* 94, 96-98; *Physician's Tale* 95-96; *Squire's Tale* 89; *Summoner's Tale* 63; *Wife of Bath's Prologue* 46; *Wife of Bath's Tale* 57, 98-99; *The House of Fame* 91, 95; *The Legend of Good Women* 10, 88-95; *Alceste* 94; *Cleopatra* 90, 92-93, 95; *Dido* 91-92, 94-95; *Lucrece* 95-96; *Medea* 90, 94-95; *Phyllis* 89-90; *Thisbe* 98; *Lenvoy de Chaucer a Scogan* 101; *Romance of the Rose* 29; *Troilus and Criseyde* 15, 46, 54, 87, 89, 107
Dolce stil nuovo 6
Donna angelicata 11
Envelope Pattern 111
Fortune's Wheel 43, 63-64
"Foweles in the frith" 38-39, 41, 109-10
Genius 7, 20-25, 56, 58
Goldsmith, Oliver *The Vicar of Wakefield* 94
Gower, John (general) 1-3; *Confessio Amantis* (general) 1-3, 5-18, 87, 103-5, 108-9; Structure 5, 19-31, 103-4, 109; Translations 1; Latin Marginalia--Book One 7, 23; Book Four 8; Book Seven 106; Book Eight 15, 25; Prologue (general) 5, 7-9, 15, 21, 23, 36-38, 46; Tale of Nebuchadnezzar's Dream 35-36, 48; Book One (general) 8-9, 11-14, 22-24, 27, 43-46, 53-59, 64, 66-68; Tale of Acteon 40; Tale of Florent 39-41, 43-44, 57-58, 67-68, 97-99; Tale of Mundus and Paulina 39-40, 43-44; Tale of Nebuchadnezzar's Punishment 56; Tale of the Three Questions 56; Tale of the Trump of Death 48; Tale of the Trojan Horse 62; Book Two (general) 12, 24, 27, 49-50, 63-66; Tale of Acis and Galatea 50; Tale of Constance 46, 58, 96-98; Tale of Constantine and Silvester 48; Tale of the False Bachelor 57; Tale of the Travellers and the Angel 62; Book Three (general) 12, 24, 27, 39, 45-46, 48, 50; Tale of Alexander and the Pirate 43, 100; Tale of Athemas and Demephon 39; Tale of Canace and Machaire 46-47; Tale of Namplus 46, 76; Tale of Phebus and Cornide 99-100; Tale of Piramus and Tisbee 98; Book Four (general) 12-13, 24, 33, 47-48, 54; Tale of Ceïx and Alceone 50, 91-92; Tale of Demophon and Phillis 89-90; Tale of Icarus 47; Tale of Phaeton 47, 49; Tale of Philemenis 42; Tale of Rosiphelee 63; Tale of Saul 62; Tale of Ulysses 20, 109; Book Five (general) 5, 9-10, 12-13, 24,

27-29, 41-42, 45, 55-56, 61; Tale of Jason and Medea 92-94; Tale of the King and his Steward's Wife 67; Tale of Midas 62; Tale of Paris and Helen 45; Tale of Tereus 63; Tale of Ulysses 20, 49, 109; Book Six (general) 12, 24-25, 27, 40, 67; Tale of Galba and Vitellius 62; Tale of Ulysses 20, 49, 109; Book Seven (general) 5, 8-9, 24-29, 66; Tale of Alceste 21, 26, 89, 94-95; Tale of Apame 26, 94-95; Astronomy 46; Tale of David 50; Tale of Gideon 50; Tale of King, Wine, Woman, and Truth 21, 26, 94; Tale of Lichaon 35, 38; Tale of Lucretia 95-96; The Planets 35; Tale of Tobias and Sara 96; Tale of Virginia 34, 95-96; Book Eight (general) 7-8, 11, 13-16, 21-22, 24-25, 34-36, 46, 51, 56, 60, 85-86, 93-94, 101; Rhyme Royal 7; Laws of Marriage 22; Meditation on England 22; Origin of Mankind 22; Prayers for England 22; Tale of Amon 22; Tale of Appolinus of Tyre 21-23, 25, 41, 44-45, 59-69, 73-85, 88, 98, 112-13; Tale of Caligula 22; Tale of Cleopatra 92-93, 95; Tale of Lot and his Daughters 22; "To King Henry IV: In Praise of Peace" 36; *Mirour d'Omme* 5, 27-28, 55; *Vox Clamantis* 5, 74-75, 89, 107

Italian Authors   Boccaccio 10, 19, 91, 107; Dante (general) 22; English familiarity with 105-7; *Convivio* 107; *De Monarchia* 106; *Divina Commedia* 9, 13, 45, 106, 108; *Vita Nuova* 5-14, 16-17, 103, 105-8

Jongleurs 53

Juncture 20, 24-25

King Horn 40, 53-54

Langland, William *Piers Plowman* 31, 34, 43, 49, 56, 58, 63, 71

Latin Authors and Works   *Apollonius of Tyre* 59-61, 69, 74, 77-85, 88, 112; Augustine   *De Civitate Dei* 95; Boethius   *De Consolatione Philosophiae* 5, 37; *Carmina Burana* 110; Gotfried von Viterbo *Pantheon* 59-61, 69, 77, 79, 84, 111-12; Livy 95; Ovid *Heroides* 91, 93, 95; *Metamorphoses* 5, 40, 75, 91-92, 95, 99, 103; *Ovide Moralisée* 99; Virgil 74, 91, 95

Love 5-17, 27-28, 30, 65; 108; *Amor* and *Caritas* 10-11, 15, 17, 26, 30, 65-66, 85, 108; *Fin'Amor* 30, Fire of Love 49-50

Lydgate, John *Life of Saint Alban and Saint Amphibal* 73

Marginal Incidents 22, 26-27

Metonymy 33-34, 37-38, 44-45, 53-54, 58-59, 61, 65, 67-69, 71, 98

Middle English Lyrics 34, 72

Narremes 19-20, 22-25

Number Nine 10

Old English Works   *Andreas* 111; *Apollonius of Tyre* 74, 80-85, 112; *Beowulf* 29, 34-35, 72, 75-76, 80, 83, 85-86, 109; *Elene* 77, 81; *Juliana* 112

Old French and Anglo-Norman Authors and Works   Benoît de Sainte Maure 93; Chrétien de Troyes 30, 35, 65; Guillaume de Machaut *Voir Dit*